NEW ZEALAND
BASICS
1

T0359938

my country

my people

RUTH NAUMANN

NELSON
A Cengage Company

NZ Basics 1: My Country, My People
2nd Edition
Ruth Naumann

Cover design: Cheryl Rowe
Text design: Cheryl Rowe
Illustrations: Brenda Cantell
Typeset: Cheryl Rowe, Macarn Design
Production controllers: Jess Lovell and Siew Han Ong
Reprint: Jess Lovell

Any URLs contained in this publication were checked for currency during the production process. Note, however, that the publisher cannot vouch for the ongoing currency of URLs.

First published in 2001.

Acknowledgements
page 16 Maria Engelken

page 18,20 New Zealand Ministry of Civil Defence and Emergency Management

page 38 (Marchant's snail) Crown copyright: Department of Conservation Te Papa Atawhai (October 2010). Photo by: Duncan Toogood.

page 38 (bat) Crown copyright: Department of Conservation Te Papa Atawhai. Photo by Jane Sedgeley.

For product information and technology assistance,
in Australia call **1300 790 853**;
in New Zealand call **0800 449 725**

For permission to use material from this text or product, please email **aust.permissions@cengage.com**

National Library of New Zealand Cataloguing-in-Publication Data
Naumann, Ruth.
My country, my people / Ruth Naumann. 2nd ed.
(New Zealand basics ; 1)
Previous ed.: New House Publishers, 2001.
ISBN 978-01702-177-98
1. New Zealand—Geography—Juvenile literature. 2. New Zealand —Geography—Problems, exercises, etc.—Juvenile literature.
[1. Geography—Problems, exercises, etc. 2. New Zealand— Geography. 3. New Zealand—Geography—Problems, exercises, etc.] I. Title. II. Series.
919.30076—dc 22

Cengage Learning Australia
Level 7, 80 Dorcas Street
South Melbourne, Victoria Australia 3205

Cengage Learning New Zealand
Unit 4B Rosedale Office Park
331 Rosedale Road, Albany, North Shore 0632, NZ

For learning solutions, visit **cengage.co.nz**

Printed in Malaysia by Papercraft.
10 11 12 13 14 24

Contents

Answers: Removable section in the centre of the book

How much do you know already?

A Use the map and description to name the following.

1 closest large neighbour _____

2 ocean _____

3 sea _____

4 volcanic island _____

5 capital city _____

6 base camp at Antarctica _____

7 strait _____

8 region with a lot of fiords _____

9 highest mountain _____

10 largest city _____

11 large port _____

12 largest lake _____

13 inter-island ferry town _____

14 earthquake-damaged city _____

15 island _____

16 four main compass points

_____

_____

_____

_____

17 longest river _____

18 tourist hotel at Ruapehu _____

19 main oil and gas producing city _____

20 largest lake in the South Island _____

21 type of feature the Remarkables and Rimutakas are _____

22 land feature found at Fox and Franz Josef _____

23 tunnel near Milford Sound _____

24 kauri forest region _____

25 famous mountain chain _____

25

B Circle the best answer to finish the following statements about New Zealand.

1 The New Zealand population is closest to
  a 3.8 million **b** 4.5 million **c** 5.6 million.

2 The non-native tree is
  a rimu **b** miro **c** eucalyptus.

3 The Japanese word for harbour wave is
  a toja-san **b** tsetse **c** tsunami.

4 Bola was a famous
  a volcanic eruption **b** cyclone **c** harbour wave.

5 A low on the weather map shows
  a wonderful weather **b** bad weather **c** the forecaster is not sure.

6 New Zealand's most important trading partner in this list is
  a Japan **b** Chile **c** Tibet.

7 Geothermal power is produced in
  a Huntly **b** Wairakei **c** Manapouri.

8 Sleeping volcanoes are said to be
  a active **b** dormant **c** unreliable.

9 The most common natural hazard in New Zealand is
  a flood **b** earthquake **c** drought.

10 The mineral produced at Lake Grassmere in Marlborough is
  a salt **b** sulfur **c** clay.

11 The name of the scale which measures earthquakes is
  a Rechtmal **b** Rightson **c** Richter.

12 New Zealand is right on the edge of a Plate called
  a Atlantic **b** Tasman **c** Pacific.

13 The most popular energy used in private homes comes from
  a solar **b** wood **c** electricity.

14 New Zealand's molten rock comes from a
  a volcano **b** landslip **c** nuclear power station.

15 Project Crimson aims to save the
  a hemlock **b** pohutukawa **c** whale.

16 Stopping unwanted organisms getting into the country is known as
  a biosecurity **b** pastoral care **c** Gondwanaland.

17 New Zealand's natural hazards, for its size, are
  a many **b** few **c** too few to count.

18 Plants are known as
  a gloriana **b** davinia **c** flora.

19 Sedimentary is a type of
  a forest **b** rock **c** toothpaste.

20 The animal that was not introduced by people is the
  a pig **b** bat **c** possum.

20

NZ lies in the south-west Pacific Ocean. It is a big southern neighbour to Pacific islands such as Tonga, Fiji, Niue, Samoa, Tokelau, Cook Islands.

The nearest large land mass to NZ is Australia, 1,600 km to the west. The Tasman Sea (the ditch) lies between them.

The equator divides the world into two hemispheres – the Northern Hemisphere which is north of the equator, and the Southern Hemisphere which is south of the equator. NZ is in the Southern Hemisphere.

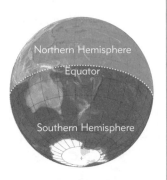

Northern Hemisphere

Equator

Southern Hemisphere

The world is divided into Time Zones. NZ Standard Time is 12 hours ahead of Co-ordinated Universal Time. Time in NZ's Chatham Islands is 45 minutes ahead of NZ.

NZ was the last large area of land in the world that humans reached and settled. Before humans, only birds, bats and insects lived in the forest.

In most other countries in the world, humans have completely changed the look of the land. But in NZ, humans have not had time to do this. For example, NZ still has trees that may have been alive over a thousand years ago. Some of these trees got to do what no European ever did – see a live moa.

NZ is closer to Asia than Europe which has led some politicians to talk about NZ being an Asian country.

NZ waters to the south are part of a special whale sanctuary. Christchurch is a main gateway to Antarctica. The Ross Dependency that NZ is responsible for is a land almost totally covered by ice. This is where NZ operates Scott Base in Antarctica.

9780170217798

Legend says the North Island – Te Ikā ā Māui – is the world's largest fish. Look at the map and you can see Wellington is the head, Cape Taranaki and East Cape are the fins, and Northland is the tail.

The world is divided into developed countries, which are those that have used their natural resources such as coal to develop industries and wealth, and developing countries (also called underdeveloped or Third World) which are still struggling to develop industries. NZ belongs to the developed countries.

1 Mark where you live on the map. Then draw arrows labelled a, b, c, d to show in which direction you'd go from your house to get to

a South America **b** Australia

c the equator **d** Antarctica.

2 Put a tick in the boxes beside statements that are correct and a cross in the boxes beside statements that are not correct.

a New Zealand time is behind Co-ordinated Universal Time. ☐

b New Zealand is in the Southern Hemisphere. ☐

c New Zealand is a Third World country. ☐

d Antarctica lies to the south of New Zealand. ☐

e Asia is closer to New Zealand than Europe is. ☐

f The ditch lies between New Zealand and Australia. ☐

g New Zealand is in the north-east Pacific Ocean. ☐

Distances

In Europe, you can whizz through several countries in a day. New Zealand does not have close neighbours like that. It is more isolated.

Signposts at Bluff at the bottom of the South Island, and at Cape Reinga at the top of the North Island, point in all directions across the sea to show how many thousands of kilometres away places such as New York and London are.

The diagram shows some approximate distances between Wellington, New Zealand's capital city, and other places in the world.

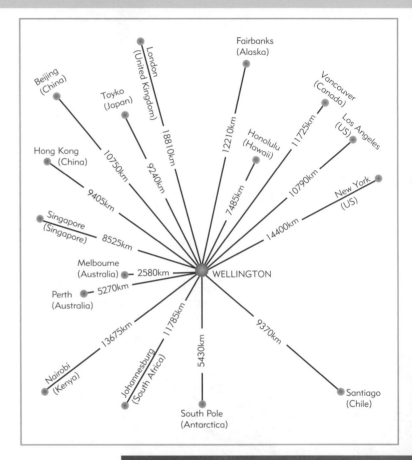

1 ▷ Write in the missing figures:

a Wellington – Los Angeles _____ km.

b Nairobi – Wellington _____ km.

c Santiago – Wellington _____ km.

d Wellington – the South Pole _____ km.

e Beijing – Wellington _____ km.

f Wellington – Vancouver _____ km.

2 ▷ Circle the smallest distances in each of the following pairs.

a (i) Wellington – Fairbanks   or   (ii) Wellington – Perth

b (i) Tokyo – Wellington   or   (ii) Beijing – Wellington

c (i) Wellington – Singapore   or   (ii) Wellington – Johannesburg

3 ▷ Circle the biggest distances in each of the following pairs.

a (i) Melbourne – Wellington   or   (ii) Hong Kong – Wellington

b (i) Honolulu – Wellington   or   (ii) New York – Wellington

c (i) Singapore – Wellington   or   (ii) South Pole – Wellington

9780170217798

Size

New Zealand has two main and a number of smaller islands.

The North and South Islands are separated by Cook Strait. It is 20 km wide at its narrowest point. A 13-year-old schoolgirl recently swam across it.

Stewart Island is about 30 km south of the South Island.

As well as the main and nearby islands, New Zealand includes these small, inhabited (lived on), outlying islands: the Chatham Islands (850 km east of Christchurch), Raoul Island (930 km north-east of the Bay of Islands), Campbell Island (590 km south of Stewart Island).

New Zealand is about 1,600 km long and 450 km wide at its widest point. Its coastline, 5,650 km long, is the seventh longest coastline of any country in the world.

The town furthest from the sea in New Zealand is Cromwell which is about 120 km away.

New Zealand's highest point is Aoraki (Mt Cook) at 3,754 metres.

Its lowest point is in Lake Hauroko in Fiordland at 306 metres below sea level.

New Zealand also looks after Tokelau (3 small atolls in the South Pacific) and the Ross Dependency (in Antarctica).

Land Area	Size (square kilometres)
North Island	113,729
South Island	150,437
Offshore islands*	1,065
Stewart Island	1,680
Chatham Islands	963
Raoul Island	34
Campbell Island	113
*Includes those 20 sq km or larger except those mentioned in the list.	

1 Name the New Zealand islands marked on the map.

a _____

b _____

c _____

d _____

e _____

f _____

Pacific Ocean

2 Say which measurements the following stand for. (The last one is tricky.)

a 3,754 m _____

b 20 km _____

c 963 sq. km _____

d 5,650 km _____

e 450 km _____

f 1,680 sq km _____

g 306 m _____

h 30 km _____

i 850 km _____

j 150,437 sq km _____

k 3 _____

l 268,021 sq. kms _____

North Island regions

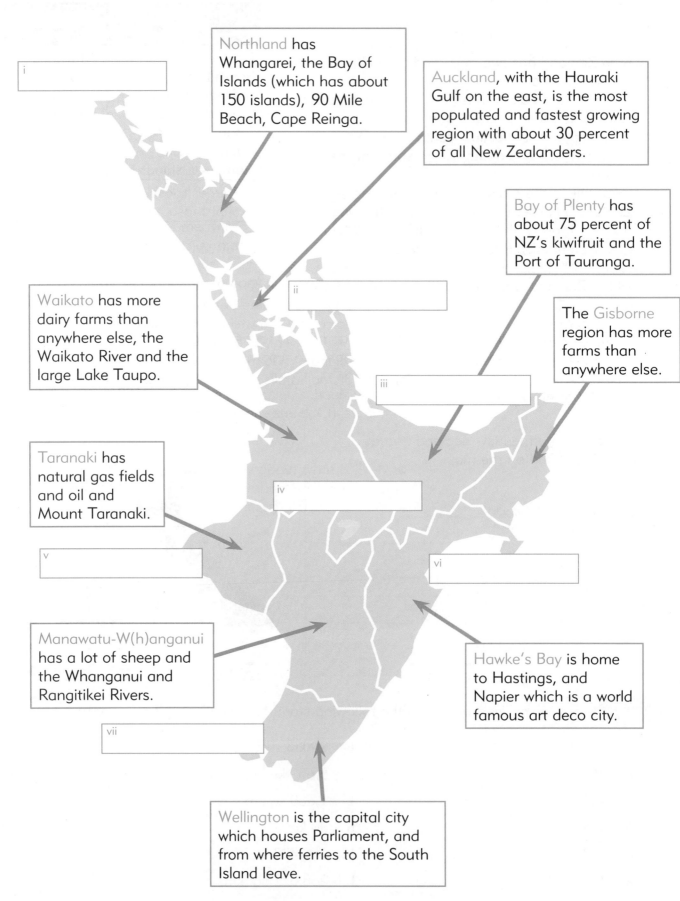

i

Northland has Whangarei, the Bay of Islands (which has about 150 islands), 90 Mile Beach, Cape Reinga.

Auckland, with the Hauraki Gulf on the east, is the most populated and fastest growing region with about 30 percent of all New Zealanders.

Bay of Plenty has about 75 percent of NZ's kiwifruit and the Port of Tauranga.

Waikato has more dairy farms than anywhere else, the Waikato River and the large Lake Taupo.

ii

The Gisborne region has more farms than anywhere else.

iii

Taranaki has natural gas fields and oil and Mount Taranaki.

iv

v

vi

Manawatu-W(h)anganui has a lot of sheep and the Whanganui and Rangitikei Rivers.

Hawke's Bay is home to Hastings, and Napier which is a world famous art deco city.

vii

Wellington is the capital city which houses Parliament, and from where ferries to the South Island leave.

9780170217798

1 Write down the name of the North Island region which best fits the following descriptions.

a most northerly region _____

b most southern region _____

c most easterly region _____

d most westerly region _____

e has a lot of art deco (a stylised form of design and decoration) _____

f has 90 Mile Beach (which is not 90 miles long) _____

g has a mountain with the same name as the region _____

2 Put the following into the blank boxes on the map.

a Tauranga Harbour

b Hawke's Bay

c Cape Reinga

d Wellington city

e Hauraki Gulf

f Lake Taupo

g Mount Taranaki

3 Put a tick in the box/es that are beside a correct statement.

a You can get to the ocean from any region without crossing another region. ☐

b Some regions have Pakeha names and some have Māori names. ☐

c The land area of all North Island regions is roughly the same. ☐

d The Whanganui and Rangitikei Rivers are further south than the Waikato River. ☐

e The Bay of Islands is a silly name because it has only a couple of islands. ☐

f A region may have more than one city in it. ☐

g Everybody in the North Island lives in a region. ☐

h Wellington is the only region that has a city with the same name as the region. ☐

4 Colour the North Island regions in using the following as clues for the colours to use.

green = capital city

purple = largest population

blue = kiwifruit

black = oil and gas

yellow = sheep country

red = art deco city

orange = dairy farms

pink = many farms

brown = beaches and islands

South Island regions

Nelson is the smallest region with part of its urban area in the Tasman Region, but it has a very busy port.

Marlborough is the largest grape producing region and is home to the world famous Queen Charlotte Sound, and Picton which is where ferries from Wellington sail to.

Tasman has the name of the Dutch explorer who sighted NZ in 1642. Home to the world's largest medium-density fibre board (board made from wood fibre) mill, and forest parks.

West Coast has a lot of coal and rain, and some gold and sites of old shipwrecks on its beaches.

Canterbury is the largest region and home to lakes Tekapo and Benmore, the Canterbury Plains and Christchurch city which an earthquake (2011) badly damaged.

Otago is home to Queenstown on Lake Wakatipu, lakes Wanaka and Hawea, and Dunedin (the 'Scottish' city).

Southland has a lot of fishing, Bluff oysters from Foveaux Strait, lakes Te Anau and Manapouri, and Fiordland which includes Milford Sound.

9780170217798

1 Write down the name of the South Island region/s which best fits/fit the following descriptions.

a includes Stewart Island _____

b have names which show their positions _____ and

_____

c has the name of an explorer _____

d is the most southern _____

e is the longest, though not the largest _____

f is home to Picton _____

g has several hundred million tonnes of coal _____

h was quake-damaged in 2011 _____

2 Colour the South Island regions in using the following as clues for the colours to use.

yellow = large with flat areas
purple = small but busy
green = trees
blue = fiords and lakes
red = grapes
black = coal
orange = Scottish influence

3 Put the names of regions or places in the gaps to best finish the following sentences.

a Joel lives in Nelson and because he likes ships, he spends a lot of time visiting the

busy _____.

b Mo loves eating Bluff oysters so much she went to live in the _____

region to be as close as possible to them.

c Ashlin still can't get used to all the rain in the _____ region because

she has come from an African desert land to live there.

d Andre is doing a project on Cook Srait ferries so it's lucky he lives in

_____where he can watch sailings every day.

e Llewellyn's cousins from Scotland felt right at home when they visited her

house in the city of _____.

f Gustavo is writing a poem about his region of _____ and has thought

of fan, can, pan, ran and tan to rhyme with it.

g Justine loves to sit at the head of Lake Wakatipu and paint a picture of the town of

_____.

h Seb likes flying in his uncle's helicopter over the region of _____ and

taking photos of the amazing and huge plains.

The 'Drifting Continents' theory

continent
a large unbroken land mass

theory
an opinion or idea that has not been proved

drifting
being carried or moved along without particular direction

Gondwana
a region in central India

The 'Drifting Continents' theory suggests that New Zealand was once part of a huge land mass.
About 200 million years ago this mass began to break into two.
New Zealand was part of the southern bit known today as Gondwanaland.
Gondwanaland also began to break up. Parts slowly drifted away from each other. They became Africa, India, South America, Antarctica, Australia, and New Zealand.
The theory says that New Zealand still drifts although only a few centimetres a year.

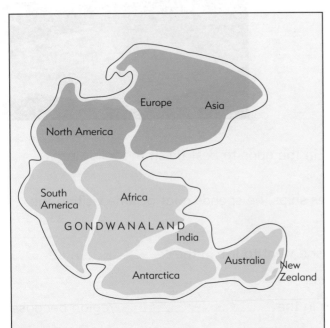

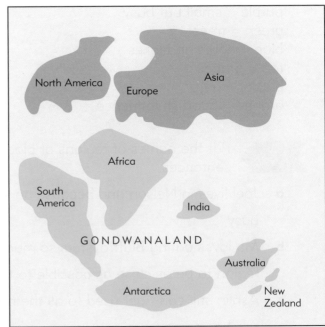

1 Finish the following sentences.

a Because it is a large unbroken land mass, Australia is called a _____.

b A theory is an idea that has not yet been _____.

c The place in India that gave its name to a giant continent is _____.

2 Tick the correct statement about the 'Drifting Continents' theory.

a New Zealand was in the northern part of the first large land mass. ☐

b The large land mass began to break up about 200 million years ago. ☐

c If New Zealand still drifts, it is only a few kilometres a year. ☐

9780170217798

UNIT 8

The 'Ring of fire'

> **tectonic**
> refers to the conditions within the Earth that cause movements of the crust

> **crust**
> the outer surface of Earth

> **plate**
> a section of the Earth's crust

Plate tectonics is the theory that Earth's crust is made of a series of rigid (rock) plates which slowly drift about. Sitting on top of the plates are the continents. New Zealand is in the area known as the Pacific Plate whereas Australia is in the area known as the Indo-Australian Plate.

The idea is that when plates such as the Pacific Plate and the Indo-Australian Plate grind against each other, earth movements such as mountains and earthquakes happen.

New Zealand is right on the edge of the Pacific Plate. This plate runs from New Zealand to Japan, to Alaska, down the American coast to Antarctica. Between it and other plates is a belt of active volcanoes and frequent earthquakes. This belt has been given the name 'Ring of fire'.

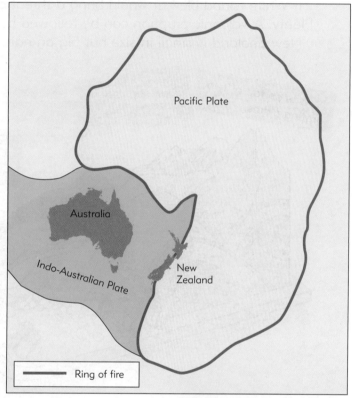

1 Write down the best word to finish the following sentences.

a The outer surface of the Earth is called _____.

b A _____ is a section of the Earth's crust as well as something you put food on.

c New Zealand is on the _____ Plate.

2 Circle the best answer for the following.

a The Ring of fire is a belt of (i) active volcanoes (ii) sleeping volcanoes.

b The Pacific Plate and the Indo-Australian Plate are (i) beside each other (ii) not beside each other.

c The tectonic plates are (i) fiery and rubbery (ii) slow and rigid.

Natural hazards

natural
made by nature rather than people

hazard
a possible danger to people

Natural hazards are the possible dangers to people, property and the environment posed by extreme events in nature such as earthquakes, droughts and floods.

Extreme natural events can create other hazards. An earthquake in hill country might set off huge landslides on farm land.

If White Island blew, it would bring a threat of a tsunami (harbour wave) to the Bay of Plenty. A volcanic eruption can be followed by months of floods.

New Zealand is small in size but big on natural hazards. This is because:

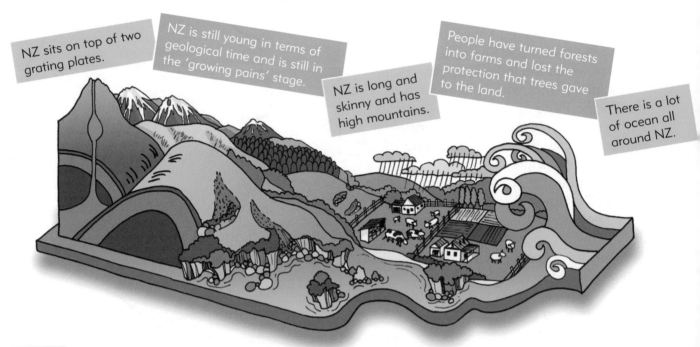

NZ sits on top of two grating plates.

NZ is still young in terms of geological time and is still in the 'growing pains' stage.

NZ is long and skinny and has high mountains.

People have turned forests into farms and lost the protection that trees gave to the land.

There is a lot of ocean all around NZ.

1 In the boxes write the name of the natural hazard shown in the picture.

a

b

c

d

e

f

g

h

9780170217798

Volcanoes

Just below the surface of New Zealand is a lot of heat. When molten or melted rock, called lava, rises to the surface, it bursts the Earth's crust and makes a hole called a volcano. Tephra is material erupted from the volcano. It includes ash which is the fine dust that can travel a long way. A lahar is a mudflow made by erupted material mixing with snow or water.

New Zealand has seven active volcanic areas, all in the North Island. They have all erupted before and might erupt again. Some are said to be dormant (sleeping) such as Taranaki.

Lake Taupo's crater, known as a caldera, was formed from a series of eruptions. The last was less than 2,000 years ago. There has never been a larger eruption anywhere else in the world since. It even threw out a lot more tephra than the famous eruptions of Krakatoa (second largest), Vesuvius (third largest) and St Helens (fourth largest) elsewhere in the world.

Volcanic areas
Kaikohe/Whangarei
Auckland
Whakaari (White Island)
Okataina (Tarawera is here)
Taupo
Tongariro (Ngauruhoe, Ruapehu and Tongariro are here)
Taranaki

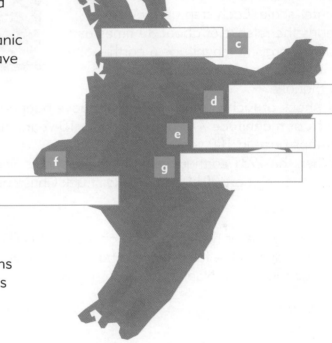

1   In the boxes on the map write the name of the volcanic areas.

2   Beside each meaning write the correct volcano words from the box.

a   hole in Earth's crust _____

b   material erupted from volcano _____

c   molten rock _____

d   mudflow _____

e   fine volcanic dust _____

f   not in action _____

g   being in action _____

h   crater formed by eruption _____

dormant
lahar
ash
volcano
active
tephra
caldera
lava

Earthquakes

An earthquake is a sudden movement in the Earth caused by a build-up of pressure which sends out shockwaves.

Earthquakes happen everywhere in New Zealand. Most are so small you never feel them.

Māori called one earthquake in Wellington (that their history says happened about 1460) 'hao whenua' – the land swallower.

Earthquake power is measured by the Richter scale. Each step up the scale means the release of about 30 times as much energy. A magnitude 6 earthquake is 30 times as large as a magnitude 5 earthquake.

A shock of Richter magnitude 6 or above happens on average about once a year, a shock of magnitude 7 or above once in 10 years, and a shock of about magnitude 8 perhaps once in 100 years.

When the 1931 earthquake hit Napier, schools were on morning break. It was lunchtime when the February 2011 earthquake struck Christchurch.

1 Write one or two words only about what is likely to happen to the following in a bad earthquake such as the one at Napier or Christchurch.

a streets _____

b ocean _____

c bridges _____

d buildings _____

e trees _____

f water pipes _____

g land _____

Strong New Zealand earthquakes

Time	Place	Magnitude Richter scale	Deaths
1843	Wanganui	7.5	
1848	Marlborough	7.1	2
1855	Wairarapa	8.1	3
1901	Cheviot	7.0	5
1914	East Cape	7–7.5	1
1929	Murchison	7.8	1
1931	Napier	7.9	17
1934	Pahiatua	7.6	256
1968	Inangahua	7.0	1
1987	Whakatane/ Edgecumbe	6.3	3
2011	Christchurch	6.3	0
			181
Compare:			
1906	San Francisco	8.25	700
1976	China	7.6	650 000

2 Unmuddle the following famous New Zealand earthquakes.

a S H R O M U N I C _____

b R R H H H C C C T I S U _____

c P R I A A W A A R _____

d H U A A A I N N G _____

9780170217798

UNIT 12

Floods and droughts

flood
overflowing water

floods can:
- kill people
- kill animals
- spread disease
- sweep vehicles from roads
- maroon people and animals
- uproot trees
- frighten people
- start landslides
- fill buildings with mud

Flooding is New Zealand's most widespread natural hazard. Rivers flooded the huts and tents of the first Pakeha settlers at Petone in 1840 and drove the settlers across the harbour to set up the town of Wellington instead.

drought
a long time without rain

droughts can:
- drop river water levels
- dry up creeks
- kill animals
- ruin farmers
- close public walkways
- cause cuts to water use
- close parks and forests
- make people depressed
- start fires
- run town water supplies low

A recent long drought in Marlborough was the worst ever recorded in New Zealand. Nelson, Golden Bay and Marlborough had almost no rain for three months. At one stage fires swept through 700 hectares of farmland near Blenheim.

Flood or drought depends on the amount of rainfall a place gets. Some rainfall examples:

Period	Amount (mm)	Place	Time
10 mins	34	Tauranga	1948
1 hour	107	Whenuapai	1966
3 months	10	Clyde	1966
6 months	53	Alexandra	1930

An annual average of 4,000 mm or more rainfall is said to be very wet. This is more to be expected in Fiordland and Westland.

500 mm or less is said to be very dry. This is more to be expected in Marlborough, Central Otago or Canterbury.

1 Use the word flood or drought to fill in the gaps in the following sentences.

a In 1966 Clyde had a _____.

b In 1966 Whenuapai had a _____.

c The most common natural hazard in New Zealand is _____.

d Places in Fiordland are more likely to have a _____ than a _____.

e In 1930 Alexandra had a _____.

f When people live along river banks they are in danger of a _____.

g Marlborough recently had a terrible _____.

h In 1948 Tauranga had a _____.

i Cleared forest can cause a _____.

j Fire risk is high during a _____.

k The early Pakeha settlers at Petone were faced with a _____.

Storms

A storm is strong winds with rain, hail or snow.

A storm in Wellington Harbour in 1968 with winds gusting up to 125 knots blew the inter-island ferry *Wahine* off course. The ferry sank and 51 people died. Stormy wind is caused by deep depressions or tornadoes.

A depression is a low pressure weather system. It is also called a 'low'. It is drawn on the weather map as circles. The closer together the circles, the stronger the wind.

A tornado is a narrow funnel of violently spinning air. A tornado in Hamilton in 1948 killed three people.

Tropical cyclones, also called typhoons or hurricanes, are storms of huge power. They form in the tropics and can move south towards New Zealand. They can change into depressions bringing heavy rainfall and gale force winds.

In 1988 Cyclone Bola affected most of New Zealand although the worst damage was in northern Hawke's Bay and the Gisborne-East Coast region.

storms can:
- cause floods and uproot trees
- kill people
- kill animals
- tear roofs off buildings
- blow down power lines
- blow vehicles off roads
- destroy farmland and crops
- smash boats in harbours
- turn freed items into missiles
- blow buildings over
- break glass
- send thunder and lightning

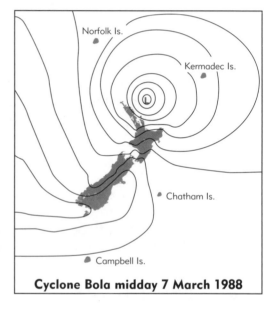

Cyclone Bola midday 7 March 1988

Norfolk Is.
Kermadec Is.
Chatham Is.
Campbell Is.

---

1 Write words in the following gaps to finish the sentences about the weather map.

a The cyclone that the weather map is about is called _____.

b The cyclone hit New Zealand in the month of _____ and the year of

_____.

c The time shown for this weather pattern is _____.

d The L stands for _____.

e Another word for L is _____.

f L is a low _____ weather system.

g The circle lines are _____ together.

h The lines show that the wind was _____.

i The cyclone travelled in a _____ direction to New Zealand from the tropics.

j Cyclones are also called _____ and _____.

9780170217798

UNIT 14

Tsunami

Tsunami is a Japanese word for harbour wave. It is a series of sea waves set off by movement on the ocean floor, such as from earthquakes or big underwater landslides, which send a lot of energy into the ocean.

Tsunami are great travellers. Even tsunami caused by earthquakes thousands of kilometres away can hit New Zealand.

In 1947 two waves, one estimated to be 10 metres high, swept onto New Zealand's coast near Gisborne. They uprooted trees and fences and destroyed buildings. They flooded a lot of lowland to a depth of 3–4 metres, killing grass and crops.

Whenever there is a strong earthquake in the Pacific area, a 'tsunami watch' begins. The map shows the time a tsunami will take to travel from any point to New Zealand.

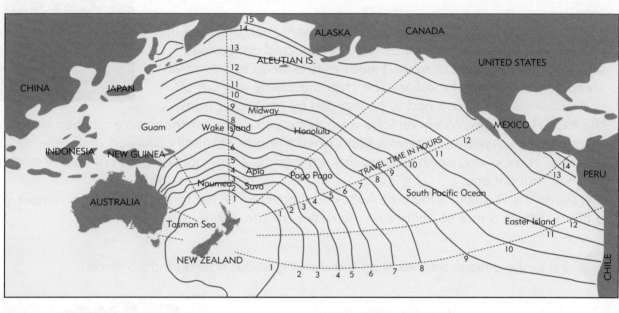

1 ▸ Give the approximate travel times in hours for a tsunami from the following points to New Zealand.

a Mexico _____   b Honolulu _____   c Noumea _____

d Apia _____   e Easter Island _____   f Suva _____

2 ▸ Write S (for silly) or W (for wise) in the box beside the following comments from people about tsunami.

a 'A tsunami would be so cool. I'd hop on my surfboard for the ride of my life.' ☐

b 'Don't know what the fuss is about. Tsunami never happen in the Pacific.' ☐

c 'If you're on the beach in a strong earthquake, don't wait to pick up your

belongings.' ☐

15 Landslips

New Zealand has many mountains, hills and slopes. Every year there are thousands of landslips. Sometimes whole hillsides give way, crushing and burying houses or pushing them down the hill. Landslips can kill people. Survivors may need to be evacuated.

Rain and landslips often go together. Rain saturates the soil and fills cracks in rocks. The land slips.

In 1846 a deadly slip buried the village of Te Rapa on the shore of Lake Taupo and killed 61 people.

Slips send large amounts of material into rivers. Normally that happens slowly and steadily over years. But events such as a cyclone can shift millions of tonnes of material in just a few days. Cyclone Bola triggered many landslips which helped wreck large areas.

In one downpour in the Wellington area, more than 300 mm of rain fell in 24 hours. This kind of flood is expected on average only once in 100 years or more. Floods metres deep roared down steep gullies, causing landslips. The Hutt motorway was cut off and hundreds of workers had to be rescued by helicopter from the roof of a factory. Many vehicles were destroyed. Some of them were crushed beyond recognition. A 3-year-old boy was killed when the side of a hall collapsed under the weight of a wall of rocks and earth slipping down a hillside. Many houses were crushed or pushed off their foundations.

A slip in the Dunedin suburb of Abbotsford covered 18 hectares. Its main movement was a 50 m slide at a rate of about one metre per minute. 69 houses were lost.

> 1 ▷ Fill in the gaps in the boxes on the drawing about how a landslip works.

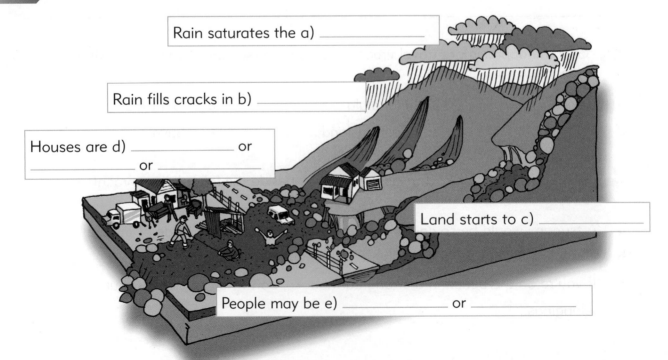

Rain saturates the a) _____

Rain fills cracks in b) _____

Houses are d) _____ or _____ or _____

Land starts to c) _____

People may be e) _____ or _____

Global warming

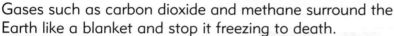

Gases such as carbon dioxide and methane surround the Earth like a blanket and stop it freezing to death.

These gases are increasing because of human activities. The blanket is getting thicker and so Earth is heating up like a greenhouse.

These processes are called

- the Greenhouse effect
- climate change
- global (worldwide) warming.

New Zealand's production of greenhouse gases such as methane from burping cows is higher than the world average.

Most, though not all, experts say global warming causes

- Earth's temperature to rise
- weather change
- some farmland to become desert
- more people in cities to die from heatstroke
- many coral reefs, which support fish, to die
- sea levels to rise
- some islands to get swamped
- crops to get smaller
- glaciers and polar ice-caps to melt
- more forest fires
- some plants and animals species to die out
- millions of people to leave their homes
- wars over water
- floods in heavily populated areas.

The good news for NZ is it is surrounded by ocean which helps cool the atmosphere, so it would probably get an increase of only a few degrees in temperature rather than the higher increase in other places.

Some coastal homes in NZ may go under.

The bad news for NZ is a lot of people live by the ocean and scientists say the ocean will rise.

NZ may get more violent storms.

Tropical diseases may increase in NZ.

Dunedin could get Auckland's climate. Auckland could get Suva's (Fijian) climate.

There may be droughts in eastern areas of NZ.

NZ may get more rain.

There may be floods in western areas of NZ.

---

1 Add the missing words to finish each drawing.

blanket of gases such as

a) _____

and b) _____

Earth

High production of greenhouse gases such as d) _____

human actions are making the blanket

c) _____

Earth heating up

New Zealand may get

e) _____

_____

_____

Features of the land

New Zealand's land shows the results of processes that have been going on over the past few million years.

braided stream – stream with channel divided into shallow waterways		**pass** – narrow way through mountains	
delta – fan-shaped silt build-up at river mouth		**plateau** – large, fairly flat area of highland; tableland	
glacier – slow-moving ice mass (or river of ice)		**rock** – a large mass of stone	
hill – a raised, rounded area of land		**scarp** – steep face hundreds or thousands of metres high	
mountain – very high land rising to a summit (top)		**valley** – low stretch of land between hills	

1 Write the correct term in each box for the land feature described.

a   Taranaki is the most climbed land feature with a summit in NZ.

b   Karangahake is a narrow valley with steep, high sides.

c   Fox is a slow-moving ice mass.

d   Many South Island rivers have channels divided into shallow waterways.

e   At Waitomo you can travel on an underground river.

f   Lake Wakatipu sits in a valley carved by a glacier.

g   White Island has erupted and could erupt again at any time.

mountain building – vast blocks of land have been squashed to form mountains and hills because New Zealand is sandwiched between the Pacific Plate and the Indo-Australian Plate.

volcanic activity – volcanic eruptions create mountains, hills, craters and lakes.

erosion – the wearing away of rock and soil by wind, water and ice.

cave – underground place opening to Earth's surface		**peak** – pointed mountain	
finger lake – lake in a valley		**ridge** – long narrow area of raised land	
gorge – narrow valley with steep sides		**saddle** – ridge shaped like a saddle between two peaks	
hot spring – spring of naturally hot water		**thermal area** – geysers and boiling mud pools	
plain – area of low, generally flat land		**volcanic cone** – cone shape made by volcanic eruptions	

h The ridge at Duffer's looks as if it's shaped for sitting in.

i The Haast lets you travel through the Southern Alps.

j The raised mound was called Coal but he couldn't see any coal around.

k Hell's Gate (Tikitere) is a wonderland of geysers and boiling mud.

l The huge mass of stone called Bottle did look a bit like a bottle.

m Hauraki's rich lowland has no high mountains.

n They chased the moa into the fan-like silt build-up at the river mouth.

Mountains

Main mountains with heights in metres	
North Island	
Ruapehu	2,797
Taranaki (Egmont)	2,518
Ngauruhoe	2,287
Tongariro	1,967
South Island	
Aoraki (Cook)	3,754
Tasman	3,497
Dampier	3,440
Silberhorn	3,300
Hicks (St David's Dome)	3,198
Lendenfeldt	3,194
Torres	3,163
Teichelmann	3,160
Sefton	3,157
Malte Brun	3,155
Haast	3,138
Elie de Beaumont	3,117
Douglas	3,085
La Perouse	3,079
Heidinger	3,066
Minarets	3,055
Aspiring	3,033
Glacier Peak	3,007

New Zealand is very mountainous. About 60 percent (16 million hectares) is over 300 metres above sea level, with 20 percent over 900 metres.

In the North Island there are ranges and volcanic peaks.

The South Island is much more mountainous than the North Island. The striking Southern Alps – Ka Tiritiri o te Moana – runs almost the length of the South Island. There are also many outlying ranges. At least 223 named peaks are higher than 2,300 metres.

Examples of ranges

North Island	South Island
Coromandel Range	Richmond Range
Kaimanawa Range	St Arnaud Range
Tararua Range	The Remarkables
Rimutaka Range	The Catlins

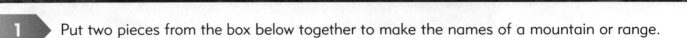

1 Put two pieces from the box below together to make the names of a mountain or range.

LINS	FELDT	KAI	DAM	ABLES	GLACIER
REMARK	PIER	TAKA	RIMU	MANAWA	CAT
LENDEN	SILBER	PEAK	HORN	LAS	DOUG

a _____ b _____ c _____

d _____ e _____ f _____

g _____ h _____ i _____

2 Write the names of the mountains alongside their heights. Turn your book sideways to do this. (Heights are in metres.)

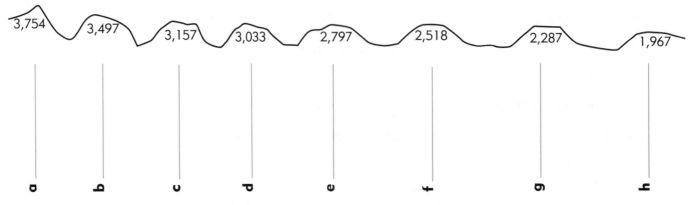

3,754   3,497   3,157   3,033   2,797   2,518   2,287   1,967

a   b   c   d   e   f   g   h

9780170217798

Plains

A plain is an area of generally flat lowland.

Canterbury, which has very high mountains, also has the largest plain in New Zealand. It is about 193 km long and 40 km wide. It took only four years for the earliest Pakeha sheep farmers to take up all the flat land to the foothills of the Alps for their farms.

Important Plains

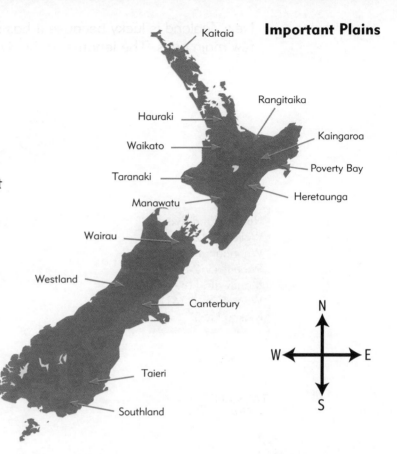

Kaitaia
Rangitaika
Hauraki
Kaingaroa
Waikato
Poverty Bay
Taranaki
Heretaunga
Manawatu
Wairau
Westland
Canterbury
Taieri
Southland

N
W — E
S

1 Give the compass direction – North, South, East or West – to finish the following sentences about where the main New Zealand plains are.

a The Taranaki Plain is in the _____ of the _____ Island.

b The Kaitaia Plain is in the _____ of the _____ Island.

c The Southland Plain is in the _____ of the _____ Island.

d The Westland Plain is on the _____ of the _____ Island.

e The Heretaunga Plains are in the _____ of the _____ Island.

f The Canterbury Plain is in the _____ of the _____ Island.

g From the Waikato Basin you go _____ to get to the Manawatu Plain.

h From Taieri Plain you go _____ to get to the Wairau Plains.

2 Colour the circle red underneath the feature that is most likely to be a plain in the following diagram.

Rivers and lakes

New Zealand is lucky because it has so many rivers and lakes. Here are a few main ones. The lengths of the rivers are in kilometres in the brackets.

Rivers

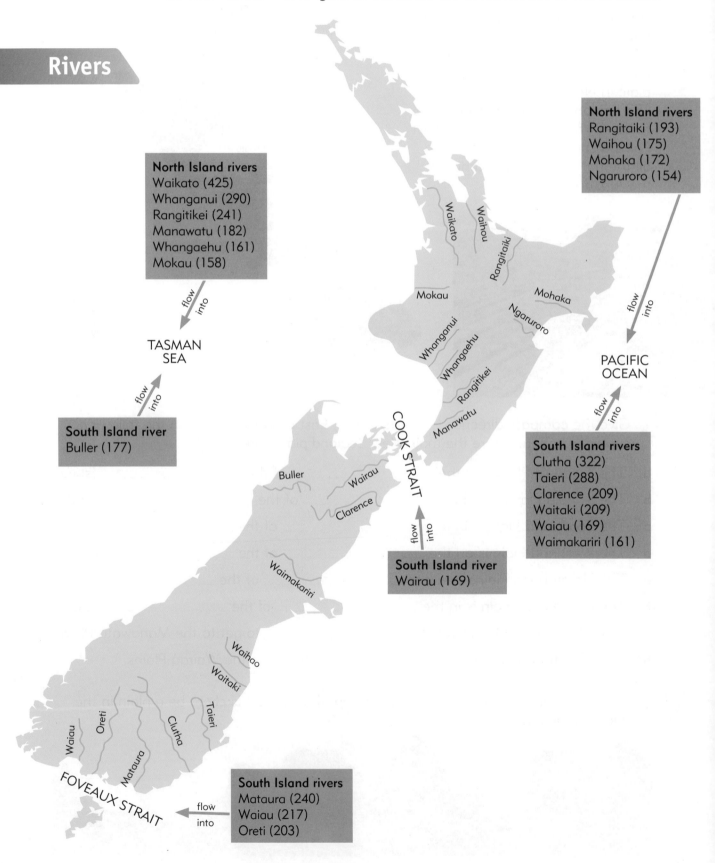

North Island rivers
Waikato (425)
Whanganui (290)
Rangitikei (241)
Manawatu (182)
Whangaehu (161)
Mokau (158)

flow into

TASMAN SEA

flow into

South Island river
Buller (177)

North Island rivers
Rangitaiki (193)
Waihou (175)
Mohaka (172)
Ngaruroro (154)

flow into

PACIFIC OCEAN

flow into

South Island rivers
Clutha (322)
Taieri (288)
Clarence (209)
Waitaki (209)
Waiau (169)
Waimakariri (161)

COOK STRAIT

flow into

South Island river
Wairau (169)

FOVEAUX STRAIT

flow into

South Island rivers
Mataura (240)
Waiau (217)
Oreti (203)

9780170217798

Lakes

The sizes of the lakes are in square kilometres in brackets.

North Island lakes
Taupo (606)
Rotorua (80)
Wairarapa (80)
Waikaremoana (54)
Tarawera (36)
Rotoiti (34)

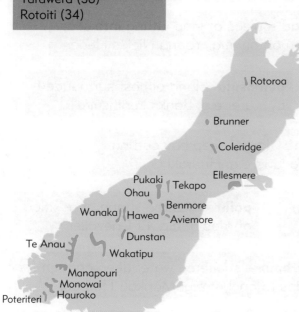

South Island lakes
Te Anau (344)
Wanaka (193)
Pukaki (169)
Hawea (141)
Benmore (artificial) (75)
Ohau (61)
Brunner (39)
Monowai (31)
Dunstan (artificial) (27)
Wakatipu (293)
Ellesmere (181)
Manapouri (142)
Tekapo (88)
Hauroko (71)
Poteriteri (47)
Coleridge (36)
Aviemore (artificial) (29)
Rotoroa (23)

1 Write in the name of the river, sea, ocean or lake to finish the following sentences correctly.

a The longest river is the _____.

b The Rangitikei river flows into the _____ Sea.

c The largest lake is _____.

d The second largest lake is _____.

e The largest artificial lake is _____.

f A South Island river that flows into the Tasman is _____.

g The shortest river out of the Mokau and the Clutha is the _____.

h A South Island river that flows into Cook Strait is the _____.

i The river closest in length to the Whanganui is the _____.

j The lake closest in size to Manapouri is _____.

k The lake that is double the size of Dunstan is _____.

l The lake closest in size to Tarawera is _____.

Features of the coast

CAPE COVE BAY ESTUARY

cove – small bay or inlet e.g. Deep Water Cove

bay – body of water almost enclosed by land but opening to the sea e.g. Goat Bay

cape – piece of land jutting out into the sea e.g. Cape Foulwind

estuary – place near wide mouth of a river where it meets sea e.g. Maketu Estuary

bar – ridge of sand in water e.g. Greymouth bar

head – piece of land jutting into sea; promontory e.g. Young Nick's Head

beach – gently sloping land at sea's edge e.g. 90 Mile Beach

peninsula – land almost surrounded by water e.g. Banks Peninsula

firth – Scottish for long inlet in seacoast e.g. Firth of Thames

gulf – large, deep bay cutting into land e.g. Hauraki Gulf

spit – narrow ridge of land projecting into the sea e.g. Farewell Spit

point – has the shape or position of a point e.g. Pt Chevalier

bight – bend in the coastline e.g. Canterbury Bight

harbour – sheltered water deep enough for ships to anchor e.g. Mankau Harbour

fiord – long, deep, narrow steep-sided inlet of sea; like Sound e.g. Milford Sound

sound – narrow channel of water e.g. Queen Charlotte Sound

strait – narrow strip of water between two pieces of land e.g. Cook Strait

bluff – a big steep cliff e.g. Twelve Mile Bluff

BAR BEACH FIRTH SPIT BIGHT FIORD

HEAD PENINSULA GULF POINT HARBOUR SOUND BLUFF

STRAIT

1 ▶ Cross out the wrong word(s) to leave the correct term.

a Land at a beach slopes gently / steeply.

b Land at Cape Kidnappers is straight / juts into the sea.

c Hauraki Gulf is a small shallow cove / large deep bay.

d Pelorus Sound is like a fiord / spit.

e Karamea Bight is straight / bent.

f Coromandel Peninsula is almost completely surrounded by water / land.

g Water is more shallow in a harbour / an estuary.

h A spit is shaped like a fist / finger.

i He knew Mako Point would look just / nothing like a point.

j Ships are more likely to get wrecked on a strait / bar.

k Another word for a promontory is a head / firth.

l To get to a beach on foot from a bluff is hard / easy.

  9780170217798

Rocks

A lot of New Zealand is rock. The oldest rocks are in Nelson, Westland and Fiordland. They have been dated back to about 570 million years ago. There are different types of rock and they have interesting names such as schist, serpentine, gabbro, gneiss and rhyolite.

New Zealand has three classes of rocks.

1 Sedimentary rocks cover almost 75 percent of New Zealand. Layered like blankets, they are rocks such as sandstone, mudstone, greywake, conglomerate and limestone formed when material like sand, bone and shell get washed into water and settle as sediment. The limestone Pancake Rocks at Punakaiki on the South Island's West Coast look like heaps of pancakes piled on top of each other. The sea has shaped them into fantastic shapes.

2 Igneous rocks are formed from volcanic eruptions. Examples are black basalt and glassy obsidian.

3 Metamorphic rocks are formed when other rocks get changed by natural heat and pressure such as earthquakes. The new rock is very hard. Limestone becomes marble, shale becomes slate.

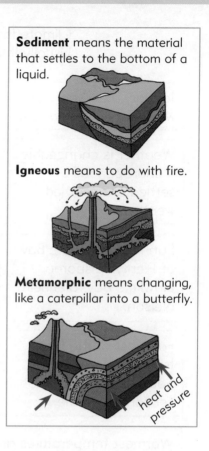

Sediment means the material that settles to the bottom of a liquid.

Igneous means to do with fire.

Metamorphic means changing, like a caterpillar into a butterfly.

1 Write in the box the class of rock formed by the following actions.

a _____

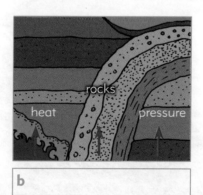

b _____

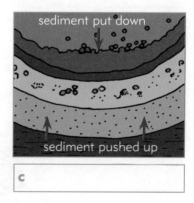

c _____

2 A 'rule' for sedimentary rocks is that in a series of layers the lowest rocks are older than those lying above them. Use the 'rule' to match the names of the rocks to their positions.

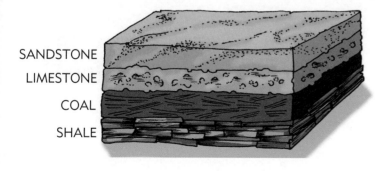

SANDSTONE
LIMESTONE
COAL
SHALE

a oldest _____

b second oldest _____

c youngest _____

d second youngest _____

Climate

Climate is the weather conditions of a place during a year.
Usually in New Zealand:

January, February are warmest; July is coldest.

Weather is changeable – short periods of settled or unsettled weather.

Sunniest areas are Bay of Plenty, Gisborne, Hawke's Bay, Blenheim, Nelson.

For most of the North Island and northern South Island the driest season is summer.

Warmest temperatures are in eastern North Island and Central Otago.

Coolest temperatures are in inland South Canterbury and Central Otago.

Driest areas are Central Otago and Canterbury.

For the West Coast of the South Island and much of inland Canterbury, Otago and Southland, the driest season is winter.

Average rainfall is from less than 400 mm in Central Otago to over 12,000 mm in the Southern Alps.

Wettest areas are Fiordland and Westland.

Climate is influenced by westerly winds, ocean, and mountains that run almost all the way through it.

Average temperatures range from 8°C – 17°C; but temperatures can go over 40 and below 0°C (Celsius).

The biggest differences between the climates of regions is west and east of the mountains.

WETTER

MOUNTAIN

DRIER

New Zealand is surrounded by ocean.

9780170217798

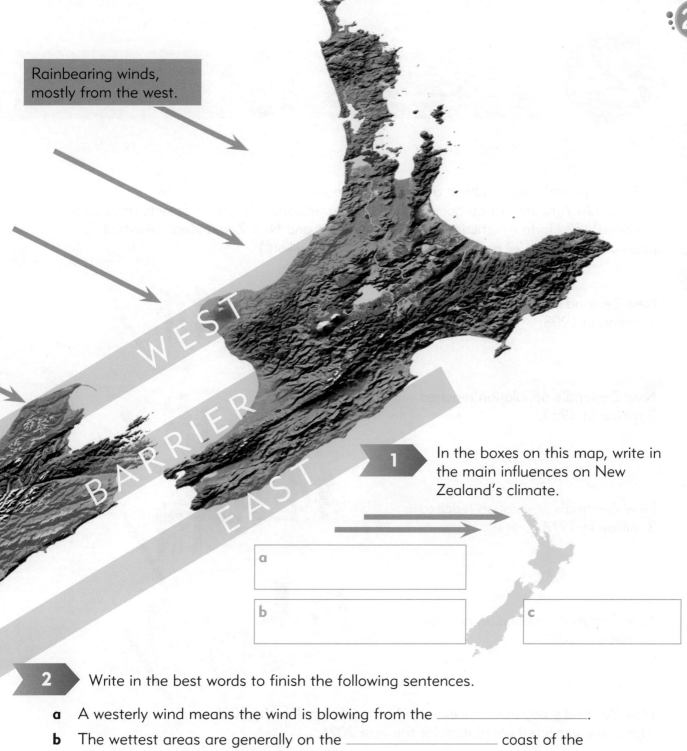

Rainbearing winds, mostly from the west.

WEST

BARRIER

EAST

1 In the boxes on this map, write in the main influences on New Zealand's climate.

a

b

c

2 Write in the best words to finish the following sentences.

a A westerly wind means the wind is blowing from the _____.

b The wettest areas are generally on the _____ coast of the _____ Island.

c The month in which lowest temperatures are recorded is most likely to be _____.

d Rainfall is measured in _____.

e Temperature is measured in _____.

f The three coolest areas are _____.

g The driest season in Northland is most likely to be _____.

h The wettest season in Bay of Plenty is most likely to be _____.

i The two sunniest areas in the South Island are _____.

j The area that can have both the warmest and coolest temperatures is _____.

k Climate is the _____ conditions of a place during a year.

Population

If the whole world was a village of just 1,000 people, it would include 584 Asians, 124 Africans, 95 Europeans, 84 Latin Americans, 55 former Soviets (including Russians), 52 North Americans, and 6 Australians and New Zealanders. (Australia's population = about 22.6 million, NZ's = about 4.4 million.)

New Zealand's population reached 1 million in 1908.

New Zealand's population reached 2 million in 1952.

New Zealand's population reached 3 million in 1973.

New Zealand's population reached 4 million in 2003.

New Zealand's population is expected to reach 5 million by 2025.
This is the expected population for the year 2026:

Ethnic group	Percentage
Māori	16
Pacific Islands	10
Asian	16
European/other	70

Note: People can identify with more than one ethnic group which means the percentages do not add up to 100.

'Population density' means the average number of people living in a square kilometre.
Some examples of population densities:

New Zealand	16	Australia	3	Chile	23
Israel	371	Japan	337	Fiji	46
Singapore	7,148	USA	32	United Kingdom	255

9780170217798

Answers

How much do you know already? – page 4

A
1 Australia
2 Pacific
3 Tasman
4 White/Whakaari
5 Wellington
6 Scott
7 Cook
8 Fiordland
9 Aoraki/Mt Cook
10 Auckland
11 Tauranga
12 Taupo
13 Picton
14 Christchurch
15 Stewart
16 north, south, east, west
17 Waikato
18 Chateau
19 New Plymouth
20 Te Anau
21 mountain ranges
22 glacier
23 Homer
24 Northland
25 Southern Alps

B 1 b, 2 c, 3 c, 4 b, 5 b, 6 a, 7 b, 8 b, 9 a, 10 a, 11 c, 12 c, 13 c, 14 a, 15 b, 16 a, 17 a, 18 c, 19 b, 20 b

Where New Zealand is in the world – page 6

2 a x b ✓ c x d ✓ e ✓ f ✓ g x

Distances – page 8

1 a 10790   b 13675   c 9370
  d 5430   e 10750   f 11725
2 a Well-Perth   b Tok-Well   c Well-Sing
3 a HK-Well   b NY-Well   c Sing-Well

Size – page 9

1 a North   b South   c Stewart
  d Campbell   e Chathams   f Raoul
2 a Aoraki/Mt Cook's height
  b Cook Strait's narrowest width
  c Chatham Island's area
  d length of New Zealand's coastline
  e New Zealand's greatest width
  f Steward Island's area
  g Lake Hauroko's low point below sea level
  h distance between Stewart and South islands
  i distance between Christchurch and Chathams
  j South Island's area
  k number of atolls of Tokelau
  l total area of New Zealand

North Island regions – page 10

1 a Northland   b Wellington
  c Gisborne   d Northland
  e Hawke's Bay   f Northland
  g Taranaki
2 i Cape Reinga   ii Hauraki Gulf
  iii Tauranga Harbour
  iv Lake Taupo   v Mount Taranaki
  vi Hawke's Bay   vii Wellington City
3 a, b, d, f, g are correct
4 green = Wellington, blue = Bay of Plenty, yellow = Manawatu–W(h)anganui, orange = Waikato, brown = Northland, purple = Auckland, black = Taranaki, red = Hawke's Bay, pink = Gisborne

South Island regions – page 12

1 a Southland   b West Coast, Southland
  c Tasman   d Southland
  e West Coast   f Marlborough
  g West Coast   h Canterbury
2 yellow = Canterbury, purple = Nelson, green = Tasman, blue = Southland, red = Marlborough, black = West Coast, orange = Otago
3 a port   b Southland
  c West Coast   d Marlborough
  e Dunedin   f Tasman
  g Queenstown   h Canterbury

The 'Driting Continents' theory – page 14

1 a continent   b proved
  c Gondwana
2 b

The 'Ring of fire' – page 15

1 a crust   b plate   c Pacific
2 a (i)   b (i)   c (ii)

Natural hazards – page 16

a storm   b volcano   c avalanche
d erosion or landslide   e drought
f flood   g earthquake   h tsunami

Volcanoes – page 17

1 a Kaikohe/Whangarei
  b Auckland   c White Island/Whakaari
  d Okataina   e Taupo
  f Taranaki   g Tongariro
2 a volcano   b tephra
  c lava   d lahar
  e ash   f dormant
  g active   h caldera

Earthquakes – page 18

1 a blocked   b drained
  c collapsed   d collapsed
  e uprooted   f twisted, burst
  g pushed up, landslides
2 a Murchison   b Christchurch
  c Wairarapa   d Inangahua

Floods and droughts – page 19

a drought   b flood   c flood
d flood, drought   e drought   f flood
g drought   h flood   i flood
j drought   k flood

Storms – page 20

a Bola   b March, 1988
c midday   d low
e depression   f pressure
g close   h strong
i south   j typhoons, hurricanes

Tsunami – page 21
1 a 12   b 9   c 2
   d 4   e 9   f 3
2 a S   b S   c W

Landslips – page 22
a soil   b rock
c slip   d crushed, buried, pushed
3 killed, evacuated

Global warming – page 23
a carbon dioxide   b methane
c thicker   d methane
e rising ocean, more tropical diseases, melting glaciers

Features of the land – page 24
a mountain   b gorge
c glacier   d braided stream
e cave   f finger lake
g volcanic cone   h saddle
i pass   j hill
k thermal area   l rock
m plain   n delta

Mountains – page 26
1 (any order) Remarkables, Kaimanawa, Silberhorn, Catlins, Glacier Peak, Douglas, Dampier, Lendenfeldt, Rimutaka
2 a Aoraki/Cook   b Tasman   c Sefton
   d Aspiring   e Ruapehu   f Taranaki
   g Ngauruhoe   h Tongariro

Plains – page 27
1 a east, North   b north, North
   c south, South   d west, South
   e east, North   f east, South
   g south   h north
2 the seventh circle from the left

Rivers and lakes – page 28
a Waikato   b Tasman   c Taupo
d Te Anau   e Benmore   f Buller
g Mokau   h Wairau   i Taieri
j Hawea   k Waikaremoana   l Coleridge

Features of the coast – page 30
a gently   b juts into the sea
c large deep bay   d fiord
e bent   f water
g estuary   h finger
i just   j bar
k head   l hard

Rocks – page 31
1 a igneous   b metamorphic   c sedimentary
2 a shale   b coal   c sandstone
   d limestone

Climate – page 32
1 a westerly winds   b ocean
   c mountains

2 a west   b West, South
   c July   d millimetres (mm)
   e degrees Celsius (°C)
   f Southland, Fiordland, Coastal Otago
   g summer   h winter
   i Blenheim, Nelson
   j Central Otago   k weather

Population – page 34
1 a Australia   b Fiji   c NZ
   d USA   e UK
2 a 70   b 1 million   c i 44 years
   ii 21 years   d 2025
   e some people belong to more than 1 group
   f ethnic   g census
   h Christchurch earthquake
   i increasing   j 2003

Cities and towns – page 36
1 a Auckland, Wellington, Christchurch
   b Invercargill   c Taupo
   d Napier, Hastings   e Whangarei
   f Gisborne   g Timaru, Oamaru
2 a Singapore   b NZ
   c Papua NG   d Samoa
   e Indonesia   f China

Land use – page 37
1 a natural forest   b planted forest
   c pasture and arable   d other
2 a 2   b 1, 4, 11
   c 1, 2, 3, 6, 7, 9   d 4, 8

Cultural features on the land – page 38
1 a South   b South   c North
   d North   e North   f South
   g North
2 level crossing, highway, church, mine, Māori Pa, cemetery
3 a road   b bridge
   c trig station   d lighthouse
   e railway station   f building
   g railway   h church

Animals – page 40
a giant weta N   b bat N
c blue duck N   d stoat/weasel I
e Hector's dolphin N   f pig I
g rat I   h moa N
i kea N   j deer I
k Marchant's snail N   l kiwi N
m rabbit I   n pukeko I
o possum I   p tuatara N

Plants – page 41
1 a kauri   b kakabeak   c kowhai
2 (any order) kauri, kakabeak, pohutukawa, karaka, kowhai, onga-onga
3 (any order) hemlock, kiwifruit, pine, pampas, banana passionfruit, wild ginger, Old Man's Beard, apple tree, potato, beans, gorse, blackberry, grasses, parsley

Forests – page 42
1 a land, 100 x 100m   b exotic
   c absorbing greenhouse gas carbon dioxide
   d grow, increase
2 (any order) beech, taraire, tawa, kahikatea, rimu, miro, matai, kauri, totara
3 (any order) pine, eucalypts, cypress, blackwood, macrocarpa, black walnut

Parks – page 43
1 a ?   b ✓   c ?
   d ✓   e ?
2 a Bay of Islands   b Hauraki
   c Kaimai-Mamaku d Te Urewera
   e Tongariro   f Egmont
   g Abel Tasman   h Marlborough Sounds
   i Westland   j Aoraki/Mt Cook
   k Mt Aspiring   l Fiordland

Farming – page 44
1 a C   b A,B   c C,B   d C   e A,B   f C
   g C   h A   i B   j A   k C   l A
   m C   n A   o C   p A   q A   r C
   s A,B t A   u B
2 a Molesworth   b dairy
   c Fonterra   d sheep

Horticulture – page 46
1 squash/kabocha, chestnuts, honey, capsicums, olives, onions, velvetines, truffles, walnuts
2 citrus – grapefruit, lemons, manderins, oranges, tangelos; pip fruit – apples, pears, Nashi; stone fruit – apricots, nectarines, peaches, cherries; berry fruit – blackcurrants, blueberries, boysenberries, raspberries, persimmons, strawberries; subtropicals – avocados, feijoas, kiwifruit, tamarillos, passionfruit, grapes

Fisheries – page 47
1 a sustainably managed
   b rock lobster   c Quota management
   d customary fishers e nautical mile
   f Australia   g Exclusive Economic Zone
2 a hoki or mussels b orange roughy
   c squid or salmon d paua
   e rock lobster

Industries – page 48
1 a primary   b tertiary   c secondary
   d tertiary   e primary   f secondary
   g secondary
2 a redundancy   b unemployment
   c organics   d information
   e film   f technology
3 a sales workers   b labourers
   c machinery operators and drivers d 22.7 (000)

Energy – page 50
1 a Transport   b Residential
   c Commercial   d Agriculture e Industrial
2 a hydro   b coal   c geothermal
   d oil/gas   e oil   f wind

Tourism – page 51
1 a average spend per person per trip
   b Kiwis employed in tourist industry
   c tourism earnings each year
   d Pure NZ marketing campaign
2 a 5   b 6   c 1   d 3   e 2   f 4

Biosecurity – page 52
1 a ✓   b ✓   c x   d x   e x
2 a living   b 1,000
   c infectious   d sniffer

Minerals – page 53
a gold, silver   b cobalt   c black
d wollastonite   e salt   f zeolite
g dolomite   h pounamu
i aggregates, clays, limestone
j arsenic   k stibnite

Exports – page 54
1 red = 3, 17, 19; blue = 2, 4, 6, 7, 8, 9, 10, 11, 12, 13, 14; yellow = 1; green = 5, 15, 18, 20; orange = 16
2 a wool   b molluscs
   c crustacean   d textiles   e dairy
   f dairy
3 a logs ...   b dairy ...   c meats ...

Imports – page 55
1 Italy, United Arab Emirates, Brunei, Russia, Qatar
2 Hong Kong, Philippines, Saudi Arabia, Netherlands, Venezuela
3 1, 3, 4, 5, 9, 10

Resource Management Act – page 56
1 Resources = air, river, soil, native bush, coast, coal, underground water, kiwi, geyser, mountain, lake, island, wetland, hot spring
   Threats = all others
2 a Act   b management   c resources

The heartland – page 57
1 from top: Tokoroa, Te Kuiti, Taihape, Reefton, Omarama, Gore
2 a inland, not on coast, near rivers or lakes; b small towns; c beside or surrounded by rivers or lakes or both; d service working communities; e railway

Underwater New Zealand – page 58
1 a Zealandia   b volcanism   c robotic arms
   d continental shelf   e subantarctic
   f Gondwana g Kermadec Arc
2 natural gas, gold, ironsand, ferromanganese, volcanic masses, sulphides

Gateway to Antarctica – page 59
1 Antarctic research offices of Italy, US, NZ; Royal NZ Air Force, Air National Guard & US Air Force stationed; themed airbridge at airport; Antarctic Centre at airport; totem pole; Botanic Gardens' Magnetic Observatory; Lyttelton refuels Antarctic

vessels; statue of Scott; art gallery shows works of Antarctic artists; university's Gateway Antarctica Centre; Antarctic festivals

2 a Robert Scott b emperor penguin
  c Scott Base   d Operation Deep Freeze
  e Lyttelton

Northern tourist hotspots – page 60

1 (from top) Cape Reinga, Waipoua, Coromandel, White Island/Whakaari, Waitomo, Rotorua, Mt Tarawera, Lake Taupo, Tongariro, Mt Taranaki

2 peninsula, cape, cliff, sea, ocean, rainforest, kauri tree, cave, limestone, volcanic plateau, glow worm, geothermal activity, hot mud pool, mountain, terrace, lake, island, range, volcano, volcanic cone, lava sculpture, crater, hot spring, river, native bush, caldera

Southern tourist hotspots – page 61

1 Moeraki, Milford Sound, Punakaiki, Kaikoura

2 water in some form eg. glaciers, lake, ocean; tourism is based around natural land features

World-famous ski areas and beaches – page 62

1 Yellow = Broken River, Cardrona, Coronet Peak, Craigieburn, Hanmer Springs, Manganui, Mt Cheeseman, Mt Dobson, Mt Lyford, Mt Hutt, Mt Olympus, Mt Potts, Ohau, Porter Heights, Rainbow, Roundhill, Temple Basin, The Remarkables, Treble Cone, Waiorau, Whakapapa and Turoa; Blue = Anaura Bay,

Awana Bay, Cathedral Cove, Coopers, Hot Water, Kaiteriteri, Karekare, Makoriri, Manu Bay, Mission Bay, Mt Maunganui, 90 Mile, Onetangi Bay, Opunake, Piha, St Clair, Sumner, Takapuna, Taylors Mistake, Wenderholm, Wharariki

2 a Cathedral Cove b Queenstown c Piha

National cycle trail – page 63

1 lack of traffic jams, spectacular scenery, good climate, decent roads

2 (any 3) attract overseas tourists, give locals business opportunities, jobs building it, revive struggling towns, promote tourist brand, alternative routes for children & workers to use to school and workplace

The value of the environment – page 64

1 a Taranaki   b dairying
  c tourism, agriculture, organic produce
  d lose NZ money from fewer exports
  e clean and green f Resource Management, Hazardous Substances and New Organisms

Why New Zealand is special – page 65

1 a blowhole   b petrified
  c black robin, takahe, kakapo   d Milford
  e Poor Knights Islands
  f Stewart Island g island of glowing skies
  h Matheson   i Waitomo Caves

2 a 58   b 13

Final challenge – page 66

1 continent	27 aluminium	52 pine, *pinus radiata*	77 imports
2 Pacific	28 cycle trail	53 people	78 shell
3 the ditch	29 Homer	54 nature	79 earthquakes
4 Southern	30 peninsula	55 3	80 nature
5 South	31 finger	56 hectare	81 White
6 Reinga	32 pass	57 Charlotte	82 flood
7 Cook	33 Southern Alps	58 Mount Cook	83 volcanic eruption
8 Foveaux	34 Tasman	59 absorb greenhouse	84 Wellington
9 Chatham	35 South	gases	85 Taupo
10 South	36 Plain	60 200	86 Richter
11 Stewart	37 Taupo	61 scampi	87 Tarawera
12 Cook	38 North	62 large	88 earthquake
13 New Zealand	39 South	63 hectare	89 drought
14 North	40 Queenstown	64 low	90 flood
15 Hauraki	41 animals	65 horticulture	91 storm
16 Plenty	42 plants	66 primary	92 tornado
17 Taranaki	43 rabbits	67 tourist	93 cyclone
18 North	44 giant weta	68 renewable	94 harbour wave
19 South	45 Hector's	69 wine	95 Dunedin
20 South	46 kauri	70 kiwifruit	96 resources
21 South	47 pohutukawa	71 Marsden	97 Auckland
22 North	48 security	72 sun	98 lake
23 million	49 foot-and-mouth	73 geothermal	99 Poor
24 population density	disease	74 gold	100 Waitomo
25 July	50 rock	75 salt	
26 global	51 arable	76 exports	

A census (official count of the population) is held every five years. The 2011 census was not held as planned because the people of Canterbury needed time to cope with the effects of the February Christchurch earthquake.

New Zealand's population is estimated to increase by one person every 10 minutes and 46 seconds.

1 Put the names of the countries whose population densities are shown on page 34, in the correct box.

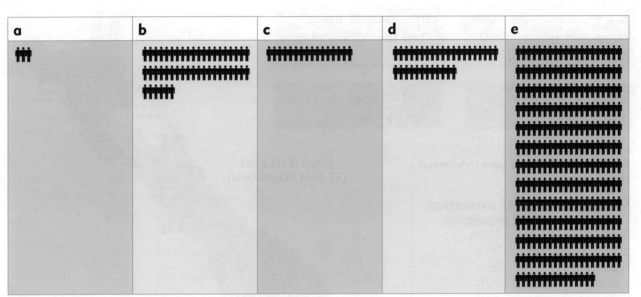

a	b	c	d	e

2 Give the following.

a The percentage of people in 2026 in New Zealand who will not be Māori, Pacific Islands or Asian. _____

b New Zealand's population in 1908. _____

c How long it took for New Zealand's population to:

   (i) increase from 1 million to 2 million people. _____

   (ii) increase from 2 million to 3 million people. _____

d When New Zealand's population is expected to reach 5 million. _____

e The reason ethnic percentages might not add up to 100. _____

_____

f The word that is used to describe 'racial' groups. _____

g The word for an official count of the population. _____

h The reason the 2011 census did not happen when planned. _____

i Whether New Zealand's population is declining or increasing. _____

j When New Zealand's population reached 4 million. _____

Cities and towns

town – urban area with some self-government such as a Council

city – a large town, often the centre of a region

urban – describing a city or town

rural – describing the countryside

Some countries and how urbanised they are

Country	Urban percentage of population
Singapore	100%
United Kingdom	90%
New Zealand	86%
Japan	79%
Indonesia	42%
China	37%
Samoa	22%
Papua New Guinea	18%

NORTH ISLAND (TE IKA-A-MĀUI)

Whangarei
AUCKLAND
Manukau
Hamilton
Tauranga
Rotorua
Taupo
Gisborne
New Plymouth
Napier
Hastings
Whanganui/ Wanganui
Palmerston North
Masterton
Nelson
Blenheim
WELLINGTON

SOUTH ISLAND (TE WAI POUNAMU)

Greymouth
CHRISTCHURCH
Timaru
Queenstown
Oamaru
Dunedin
Invercargill

STEWART ISLAND/ RAKIURA

1 Write in the names of the New Zealand cities and towns that best match the following descriptions.

a The three main centres _____, _____, and _____.

b The one closest to Stewart Island _____.

c The one closest to Lake Taupo _____.

d The two closest together (excluding the Auckland region) _____ and _____.

e The city north of Auckland _____.

f The one which would see the sun first _____.

g The two in the South Island with Māori names _____ and _____.

2 Write the name of the country beside the percentage of urban population it has.

a 100% _____   **d** 22% _____

b 86% _____   **e** 42% _____

c 18% _____   **f** 37% _____

9780170217798

UNIT 26

Land use

Before people arrived nearly 80 percent of New Zealand was covered in forest. About 14 percent was the alpine zone, and the rest was drylands, lakes and swamps.

Today 30 percent (8.1 million hectares) is in forest – 24 percent natural forest, and 7 percent planted forest; 43 percent is in pasture and arable land; 26 percent is other land.

Today people use these words to talk about land use.

pasture = land covered with grass for farm animals
pastoral = land used for grazing animals
arable = land suitable for cultivation
cultivation = working land to raise crops or farm animals
dairying = farming cattle to produce milk rather than meat
beef farming = farming cattle to produce meat
cropping = growing food crops such as wheat
market gardening = growing fruit or vegetables for sale
orcharding = food production from trees and vines.

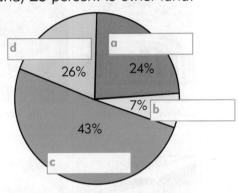

d 26%   a 24%

7% b

43%

c

Region	Main land use
1 North Auckland, Auckland	planted & native forests, dairying, sheep, beef, market gardens
2 Bay of Plenty-Waikato-Thames-Hauraki Plains	pastoral farming (mainly dairying), planted & native forest, maize, kiwifruit and other orchards
3 Volcanic plateau	planted & native forest, farming
4 East Coast-Wairarapa	sheep, market gardens, orchards, vineyards, dairying
5 Taranaki	dairying
6 Manawatu-Horowhenua	sheep, cropping, beef, planted forest
7 Marlborough Sounds-Nelson	orchards, market gardens, planted forest
8 Marlborough-Kaikoura Coast	sheep, cropping, beef, vineyards
9 West Coast	planted & native forest, dairying
10 Canterbury	cropping, sheep
11 Otago	sheep, beef, orchards, market gardens
12 Southland	sheep, beef, dairying

1 Beside the letters on the pie graph above, write what the land is used for today (planted forest, other, pasture and arable, natural forest).

2 Write down the numbers of the regions where you would most expect to see:

a escaped kiwifruit vines in native forest _____

b market gardens _____

c planted forests _____

d vineyards _____

Cultural features on the land

Cultural features are those that humans, not nature, put on the land.

Some famous cultural features

Beehive in Wellington	Sky City Tower in Auckland	Te Papa in Wellington	Auckland War Memorial Museum	Christchurch Cathedral (badly damaged in 2011 earthquake)
Auckland Harbour Bridge	Hermitage at Aoraki/ Mount Cook	Lighthouse at Cape Reinga	Hundertwasser toilets at Kawakawa	Larnach Castle in Dunedin
Chateau at Ruapheu	Mohaka viaduct	Manapouri underground power station	Eden Park rugby and cricket ground in Auckland	Shantytown at Greymouth
Māori carving	Aluminium smelter at Tiwai Point	Church of the Good Shepherd at Tekapo	Homer Tunnel at Milford Sound	Māori architecture
Treaty House at Waitangi	Pulp and paper mill at Kinleith	Ratana Church at Ratana	Stone storehouse at Kerikeri	Pania statue at Napier

9780170217798

Cultural features have special symbols on maps. Some are:

building   road   lighthouse   railway station

bridge   tunnel   trig station   church

1 Circle the correct island (North Island OR South Island) where you would find the following cultural features.

a Homer Tunnel   North Island / South Island
b Church of the Good Shepherd   North Island / South Island
c Treaty House at Waitangi   North Island / South Island
d Te Papa museum   North Island / South Island
e Hundertwasser toilets   North Island / South Island
f Hermitage   North Island / South Island
g Chateau   North Island / South Island

2 Circle the cultural features in the box.

mangroves	level crossing	sandhills	highway	swamp
mine	cave	Māori pa	river	cliff
native forest	cemetery	church	lake	mountain

3 Name the cultural features you would travel on or past if you went from A to B.

a _____
b _____
c _____
d _____
e _____
f _____
g _____
h _____

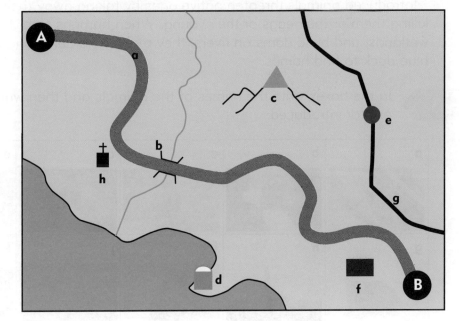

Animals

native – from a particular country	**introduced** – brought in from other countries	**extinct** – species has died out
fauna – animals of a particular country	**endemic** – native species found only in that particular country	

After people arrived in New Zealand, many birds became extinct including the flightless moa (which grew up to 3 metres high), the giant eagle and many native ducks, swans and geese. New Zealand still has the most varied seabird collection – 87 species – of any country. It still has some flightless birds such as the kiwi and weka. Some birds are protected so they cannot be hunted.

New Zealand's native animals are of great interest to the world. The tuatara is the only survivor of an ancient group of reptiles that lived on Earth at the time of the dinosaurs. The giant weta has lived in New Zealand for more than 190 million years and is the biggest insect in the world. The kakapo is the largest and rarest parrot in the world. Hector's dolphin is the smallest and rarest marine dolphin in the world. Marchant's snail is a giant carnivorous land snail only found in the North Island.

Bats are New Zealand's only native land mammals. But today New Zealand has 33 species of land mammals. Animals such as goats, possums, deer, pigs and rabbits were introduced for their fur, meat, hides and sport; animals such as cats were brought as pets; animals such as stoats and weasels were brought to control the rabbits. Others such as rats arrived as stowaways.

Introduced animals threaten native ones by taking away their food and living space, and killing them or their eggs or their young. When humans clear forests, drain swamps and wetlands, and build dams on rivers, they make it harder for natives like the black stilt and blue duck to find homes.

1 In the boxes write the names of the animals and then write either N for native, or I for introduced.

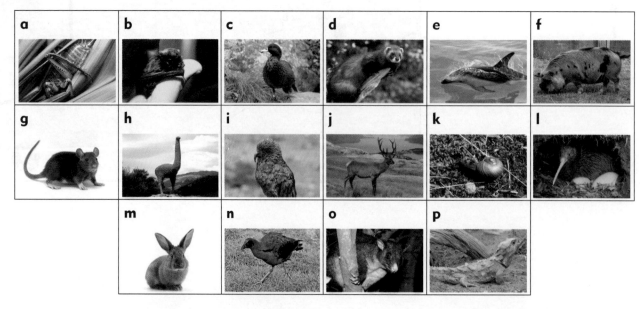

9780170217798

Plants

flora – plants of a particular country

When the islands of New Zealand drifted away from their neighbours millions of years ago, some plant species died out. New Zealand once had coconut palms, and the kauri, which now grows only in the north, once grew as far south as Canterbury.

The trees that survived are very old. Some trees, such as the largest kauri, are up to 2,000 years old which puts them among the oldest living things on Earth. The kauri is New Zealand's king of the forest. It has a huge tall trunk.

People have cut down forests and planted grasses. New plants such as apple trees, potatoes, beans, gorse and blackberry have been introduced. Other plants crept in uninvited. Today there are about 2,400 native plant species and about 2,068 introduced plants growing wild.

Introduced plants such as Old Man's Beard, escaped kiwifruit vines, banana passionfruit, and wild ginger can 'strangle' native trees. Introduced pine trees fight with natives for space but produce no food for birds. Pampas looks like native toetoe but can overrun other plants.

Some plants have become extinct such as native mistletoes and orchids. The kakabeak grows only on the East Cape where only a few are left. Its Māori name is Kowhai-ngutu-kaka and its flowers are shaped like a parrot's beak. Project Crimson is trying to save the pohutukawa, which possums are killing.

New Zealand has many poisonous plants. The leaves of the introduced hemlock and parsley look the same but hemlock is deadly even when dead and dry. Parts of the native karaka and kowhai are poisonous. Brush against the native ongo-onga and its stinging hairs will cause a violent skin reaction.

1 ▷ Write the names of the plants that are most likely to be the ones in the photos.

2 ▷ Name the native plants still around that are mentioned on this page.

a _____ b _____ c _____

d _____ e _____ f _____

3 ▷ Name 12 introduced plants mentioned on this page.

a _____ b _____ c _____

d _____ e _____ f _____

g _____ h _____ i _____

j _____ k _____ l _____

Forests

Native forest.

Native forest is called indigenous. Examples of native trees are beech, taraire, tawa, kahikatea, rimu, miro, matai, kauri, totara.

Exotic forest is not native; people have brought the trees in from another country and planted them. Examples of exotic trees are black walnut, blackwood, macrocarpa, pine, cypress and eucalypts (gums).

Little logging is done in native forests today. Most logging is in planted (exotic) forests which grow quickly in comparison to native trees.

Most planted forest is radiata pine (*Pinus radiata*). New Zealand has 1.7 million hectares of plantation forest. A hectare (ha) is 100 x 100 metres – about the size of two rugby fields.

Forestry expects to be New Zealand's leading export (goods sold overseas) by 2025. China is demanding more and more logs.

Planting trees is good for the environment because they absorb (take in) harmful greenhouse gases. It takes 20 trees to build an average house frame. This frame will have absorbed 9.5 tonnes of carbon dioxide from the atmosphere.

Exotic forest.

1 Finish the following sentences.

a A hectare measures _____.

b Today most timber production comes from _____ forests.

c Trees help the environment by _____.

d Forestry is expected to _____ in importance.

2 Write down the indigenous trees mentioned on this page.

a _____ b _____ c _____

d _____ e _____ f _____

g _____ h _____ i _____

3 Write down the exotic trees mentioned on this page.

a _____ b _____ c _____

d _____ e _____ f _____

9780170217798

Parks

New Zealand has millions of hectares set aside for parks and reserves so they can be protected and everyone can enjoy them.

World Heritage areas are the areas listed as the most outstanding natural and cultural places on Earth. There are only a few hundred in the world. Three of them are in New Zealand:

- Te Wahipounamu (includes Fiordland, Westland, Mt Aspiring and Mt Cook national parks).
- Tongariro National Park (first National Park in the world to be given to the country by a native people).
- Subantarctic Islands (includes Auckland, Campbell, Snares, Bounty and Antipodes Islands).

Te Urewera National Park (Lake Waikaremoana, Māori history)

Egmont National Park (centred around Mt Taranaki)

Marlborough Sounds Maritime Park (Queen Charlotte walkway)

Abel Tasman National Park (coastal park near Nelson, caves)

Westland National Park (high Alps, wild coast, glaciers)

Tongariro National Park (alpine park, active volcanoes)

Fiordland National Park (wilderness, fiords, Milford Track)

Kaimai-Mamaku Forest Park (near Tauranga, Rotorua and Hamilton)

Hauraki Gulf Maritime Park (47 islands on Auckland's doorstep)

Aoraki Mount Cook National Park (alpine park, highest mountain, longest glacier)

Mt Aspiring National Park (alpine wilderness, Queenstown, Wanaka, Haast)

Bay of Islands Maritime and Historic Park (islands, bays, beaches, mangroves)

1   Put ticks in the boxes beside facts (statements that are true and can be proved), and question marks in the boxes beside opinions (statements that not everyone might agree with).

a   Te Wahipounamu is the best forest and mountain wilderness in the world. ☐

b   Te Wahipounamu is in the south-west of the South Island. ☐

c   The kahikatea forests should not be part of Wahipounamu. ☐

d   Māori gave Tongariro National Park to the nation. ☐

e   Giving Tongariro National Park to the nation was a cool thing to do. ☐

2   Use the descriptions of the parks to help you write the names of the parks in the correct boxes on the map above.

Farming

Farming has always been a main money-earner for New Zealand.

One hundred years ago New Zealand farms carried just sheep and cattle to produce sheep meat, beef, wool, dairy produce and hides. Today farms might carry deer, goats, ostriches, emus, llamas, alpacas, water buffaloes and bees.

Although New Zealand still has many millions more sheep than people, dairy farming has overtaken sheep farming in importance. It earns New Zealand billions of dollars each year.

Fonterra, owned by thousands of New Zealand dairy farmers, is the world's largest dairy exporter. Much of New Zealand's milk is turned into products such as milk powder and butter for export.

Molesworth Station, in Marlborough, is New Zealand's largest cattle station. It has over 180,000 hectares.

An important issue for New Zealanders is people from other countries wanting to buy New Zealand land. Examples are Chinese and German investors.

New Zealand farming patterns

HIGHLAND

Mountains, snow, steep hills, tussock, wide streams, thin soils = sheep (wool), beef cattle.

HILLY LAND

Hills, rolling downs, planted pasture, rivers and streams, reasonable soil = sheep (wool and meat), forestry, beef cattle.

LOW LAND

Flat land, rivers and streams, rich soils = dairying, forestry, cropping, horticulture.

Also on hilly land and lowland = some deer, goat, poultry, pig, ostrich, emu, llama farms.

Extensive pastoralism = farming large areas with less labour and expense than intensive farming – very large farms and stations; few fences or hedges; low production per hectare; outback roads (sometimes aircraft used); few people per hectare; isolated from neighbours.

Semi-intensive pastoralism = farming with more cultivation and aids such as fertilisers to get the most out of each hectare; medium-sized farms; fences and hedges; paddocks; high production per hectare; good roads; average number of people per hectare; neighbours sometimes visible.

Intensive pastoralism and cropping = heavy cultivation of soil with many aids such as sprays to get the most out of each hectare; small properties; many fences, hedges and shelter belts; very high production per hectare; first-class roads; high number of people per hectare; neighbours often visible and heard.

9780170217798

1 On the illustration below, put in drawings and write in the letters to show in which area you would most expect to find each of the following. The ones marked with an asterisk belong in two areas.

a wheat	**b** sheep*	**c** forestry*
d rich soil	**e** shearing sheds*	**f** a lot of houses
g milking sheds	**h** outback roads	**i** most sheep per hectare
j a plain	**k** intensive pastoralism	**l** thin soil
m market gardens	**n** extensive pastoralism	**o** irrigation from river
p tussock	**q** vast empty spaces	**r** intensive cropping
s beef cattle*	**t** snow	**u** semi-intensive pastoralism

A

B

C

2 Circle the largest in the following pairs.

a **Station**: Nokomai / Molesworth

b **Earner**: dairy / sheep

c **Company**: Fonterra / Synlait

d **Number**: sheep / alpacas

Horticulture

Some fruit planted in New Zealand
apples
oranges
boysenberries
passionfruit
grapefruit/goldfruit
pears
peaches
apricots
kiwifruit
blueberries
tangelos
avocados
cherries
mandarins
feijoas
strawberries
grapes
lemons
Nashi (Asian pears)
raspberries
plums
tamarillos
nectarines
blackcurrants
persimmons

Horticulture is the commercial cultivation (growing for sale) of fruit, vegetables, flowers, and nuts. In recent years there has been a big jump in the area planted in horticulture.

Other countries recognise that New Zealand produces safe and high-quality food. Under New Zealand growing conditions asparagus can grow 20 cms in 24 hours.

New Zealand is a big exporter of fresh, canned and frozen fruit and vegetables. There is a growing market for organic produce (grown without chemical sprays).

Kiwifruit is a big earner. New Zealand is a world leader in kiwifruit. ZESPRI International is the world's largest marketer of kiwifruit.

For a long time, Kiwis were not interested in wine. In 1932 they drank just half a bottle a year per person. In recent years viticulture (wine industry) has taken off.

New Zealand's food technology is also famous. New Zealand scientists pioneered avocado oil. New Zealand's Plant and Food Research recently bred a new pear called Velvetine.

Do you know the most popular vegetable in New Zealand?

Tomato. Technically it is a fruit but recorded for statistics as a vegetable because it is mostly used in savoury foods.

---

1 Colour in the horticultural products you could grow or buy as food.

olives	peonies	squash/kabocha	orchids
tulips	honey	onions	chestnuts
truffles	sandersonias	capsicums	velvetines
lilium bulbs	calla lilies	walnuts	nerines

2 Draw the correct symbols into the chart above beside the types of fruit planted in New Zealand. Colour the symbols the colour shown in brackets.

citrus fruit (orange) stone fruit (red) subtropicals (green)

pip fruit (yellow) berry fruit (purple)

9780170217798

Fisheries

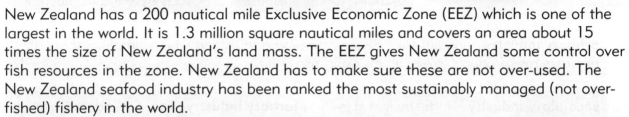

A nautical mile is about 1.85 km.

New Zealand has a 200 nautical mile Exclusive Economic Zone (EEZ) which is one of the largest in the world. It is 1.3 million square nautical miles and covers an area about 15 times the size of New Zealand's land mass. The EEZ gives New Zealand some control over fish resources in the zone. New Zealand has to make sure these are not over-used. The New Zealand seafood industry has been ranked the most sustainably managed (not over-fished) fishery in the world.

There are more than 1,000 species of fish in New Zealand's waters, some living more than a kilometre below the surface. For example, there are about 112 species of sharks. About 130 species are important for New Zealand's fish trade.

About 90 percent of all New Zealand seafood by value is exported. Surveys show 88 percent of New Zealanders eat fish at least once a month.

Top 10 export species		Top 10 export markets	
For a recent year. Brackets contain value to New Zealand ($ million).			
rock lobster	($229 m)	Australia	($286 m)
hoki	($172 m)	Hong Kong	($250 m)
mussels	($171 m)	China	($200 m)
squid	($89 m)	USA	($178 m)
salmon	($86 m)	Japan	($129 m)
paua	($63 m)	South Korea	($49 m)
orange roughy	($49 m)	Spain	($44 m)
jack mackerel	($43 m)	Germany	($43 m)
ling	($42 m)	Singapore	($40 m)
tuna	($38 m)	France	($28 m)

Who catches them?
Commercial fishers are people who fish for a living, often in trawlers. There is a Quota Management System which has rules about the number and size of fish taken.
Recreational fishers are people who fish for fun or food. Rules set limits on sizes and amounts that each person can take.
Customary fishers are tangata whenua (Māori). They can get permits to gather kai for special times such as a hui.

1 Write the correct names in the following spaces.

a used but not over-fished _____

b top fish export _____

c system with rules for commerical fishers _____

d Māori gathering kai for special times _____

e measurement used for sea distances _____

f New Zealand's top export fish market _____

g New Zealand manages fish resources in this zone _____

2 Put the names of the fish whose values best match the graph measurements, in the 'boxes'.

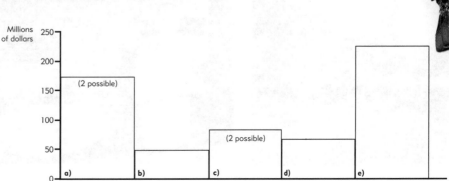

Millions of dollars

250
200
150
100
50
0

(2 possible)

(2 possible)

a) b) c) d) e)

Industries

| **industry** – a manufacturing business | **manufacturing** – making goods by hand or machine |

primary industry – industry like mining, farming and fishing which simply gathers or harvests raw products like coal, milk and fish

| **secondary industry** – industry like steel which changes raw products into manufactured goods like pots and pans | **tertiary industry** – service industry like banking and waitressing that does not produce goods but gives a service |

Once just about everyone could get a job in New Zealand. Today there is some unemployment (people unable to find jobs) and redundancy (people losing jobs because they aren't needed).

New Zealand is not a heavily industrialised country but the number of manufacturing businesses is growing.

Here are some occupations you might do that were not around in earlier days:

- food technology (e.g. speciality luxury icecream and gluten-free foods)

- titanium products (e.g. the latest laptops and mobile phones)

- film (New Zealand's film industry has been called one of the world's wonders)

- medical research (e.g. invention of world's first premature baby cooling cap)

- aircraft painting (new state of-the-art facility in Hamilton)

- creative (e.g. digital content and screen production)

- clean technology (to help the world's environment)

- aviation engineering (using New Zealand's practical approach to problem-solving)

- fashion (e.g. Karen Walker and Trelise Cooper)

- advanced materials (e.g. plastics)

- education (New Zealand is a world leader in teacher training and research)

- oil, gas and petrochemical production (Taranaki is New Zealand's energy centre)

- biotechnology (world-class biological research e.g. farming and human health).

9780170217798

1 Circle the type of industries (tertiary, secondary or primary) these people work in.

a Selena is a sheep-farmer.	primary	secondary	tertiary
b Api is a barman.	primary	secondary	tertiary
c Nicky is a factory worker.	primary	secondary	tertiary
d Fran is a web site designer.	primary	secondary	tertiary
e Mathew is a tuna fisherman.	primary	secondary	tertiary
f Riki is a printer.	primary	secondary	tertiary
g Marianna is an organic wine maker.	primary	secondary	tertiary

2 Write in the best word to finish the following sentences.

a Alex lost his job to a machine and was given a _____ package.

b Sly signed up with an _____ agency to help him find a job.

c Beth was into _____ because she gardened without using pesticides.

d Carlos worked in the _____ technology industry as a web page designer.

e Jane joined the _____ industry when she scored a job on the *Lord of the Rings* movies.

f Tony worked in the food _____ industry as a snack-food creator.

3 Use the following chart to give answers for **a** to **d**. The chart is for one recent year.

Youth employment by occupation (000)			
Managers	22.7	Technicians and trade workers	43.9
Sales workers	67.8	Communication and personal	
Machinery operators and drivers	13.3	service workers	43.5
Labourers	63.6	Clerical and administration	
Professionals	32.9	workers	28.6

a the most common occupation

_____

b the second most common occupation

_____

c the least common occupation

_____

d the number of managers

_____

Energy

renewable energy – renews itself, so it will not run out e.g. wind; renewable energy = sustainable energy	**non-renewable energy** – does not much renew itself, so it will run out e.g. coal

New Zealand needs a good supply of energy to power vehicles, buildings, industries, farms and homes. It is an energy-rich country because it has so many energy resources. Most of New Zealand's electricity comes from renewable sources so it is a leading country for sustainable energy.

oil gas	Main oil and gas reserves are in New Plymouth such as the Kapuni and Maui offshore fields; the only oil refinery is at Marsden Point near Whangarei; most oil has to be bought from overseas.
geothermal	Underground steam produces electricity e.g. Wairakei.
hydro	Electricity from river dams e.g. Manapouri.
coal	Mainly around Huntly in the North Island and Southland and the West Coast in the South Island; 2010 Pike River coal mine on West Coast explosion killed 29 workers.
wind	New Zealand is recognised as having one of the best wind resources in the world e.g. Hau nui wind farm in Wairarapa.
solar	Becoming more popular as people want to lower their bills and help the environment.

1 Fill in the pie graph with the names of the energy sectors shown for one recent year of energy use in New Zealand.

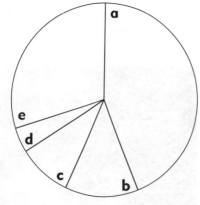

Sectors

4.3%	Agriculture
30.0%	Industrial
44.0%	Transport
12.6%	Residential
9.1%	Commercial

2 Name the type of energy most associated with the following places.

a Manapouri _____   **b** Huntly _____

c Wairakei _____   **d** New Plymouth _____

e Marsden Point _____   **f** Hau nui _____

9780170217798

Tourism

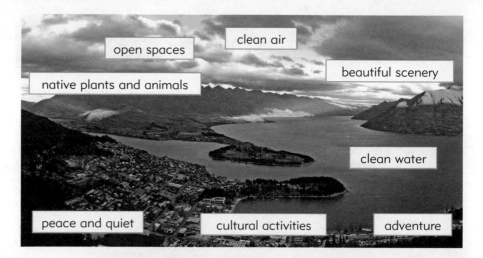

open spaces

clean air

native plants and animals

beautiful scenery

clean water

peace and quiet

cultural activities

adventure

New Zealand is famous for its natural beauty and tourism is a big industry. More than two and a half million visitors every year come to experience ➡

A tourist is a person who travels for pleasure, business or education. Local and overseas tourists can have many experiences in New Zealand such as ➡

whale watching, mountain bike trails, bungy jumping, flying-by-wire, white water rafting, helicopter skiing, jet boating, tramping, fishing, farm stays, marae visits, museums, art and craft galleries, wineries, historic buildings, shopping, festivals, cultural celebrations, food, clothing, glacier hikes, caving, mountaineering, sky diving, snow boarding, surfing.

New Zealand was the first country in the world to set up a special government department to deal with tourism. A recent global marketing campaign was '100% Pure New Zealand.' Tourism is one of New Zealand's largest export industries. It employs nearly one in ten New Zealanders. It earns billions of dollars each year.

Even a global financial crisis does not stop people from travelling for a holiday or to a special event such as the 2011 Rugby World Cup. Average spending per person per trip is over $2,500.

Key markets are Australia, UK, USA, China, Japan, Germany, South Korea and Canada.

1 Show what the following refer to.

a $2,500 _____

b 1 in 10 _____

c billions of dollars _____

d 100% _____

2 In each box write the number of the description that best fits the term.

a ☐ tourist department **d** ☐ bungee jumping

b ☐ marae visit **e** ☐ jet boating

c ☐ tourist **f** ☐ marketing campaign

① traveller
② hurtling through canyons
③ trusting in cords
④ 100% Pure New Zealand
⑤ world's first
⑥ cultural experience

Biosecurity

| **bio** – living things | **security** – keeping things safe | **organism** – any living animal or plant |

Biosecurity is about stopping pests and diseases getting in to New Zealand.

Reasons for biosecurity

- New Zealand's plants and animals are already among the most threatened in the world. About 1,000 are on the danger list. New Zealanders have a duty to stop any more unwanted 'killers' coming in.
- Tourists like visiting a New Zealand that is free from dangers such as snakes and deadly spiders. They also want to see native plants and animals.
- New diseases can impact on animal and human health. In 2001 an outbreak of foot-and-mouth in the UK resulted in over 10 million sheep and cattle being killed to stop the disease spreading. Many things, such as saliva, clothes, feet, vehicles, wind and grass can carry it and it posed a biosecurity threat to New Zealand. The Biosecurity Minister said New Zealand was to tighten its border, screen all luggage, bring in new machines to find illegal fruit and meat, and put in more teams of sniffer dogs at airports.
- New pests and diseases can impact on New Zealand agriculture, horticulture and forestry. The Varroa bee mite has slipped in and threatens New Zealand honeybees. The gypsy moth is a big international worry because it damages trees. Biosecurity has found it on cars coming into New Zealand. In 1996 the tussock moth was found in Auckland. This was a big threat to New Zealand trees, shrubs and horticulture products. Aerial and ground spraying finally got rid of it.

Varroa mite

---

1 Put a tick or a cross in the boxes to show whether each statement is true or false.

a   New Zealand has a special Biosecurity Minister. ☐

b   The Varroa bee mite is one unwanted organism that got past border controls. ☐

c   New Zealand is safe from ever being infected with foot-and-mouth disease. ☐

d   New Zealand is the only country worried about the gypsy moth getting in. ☐

e   Auckland was sprayed to get rid of the gypsy moth in 1996. ☐

---

2 Write in the gaps to best finish the following sentences.

a   'Bio' means _____ things.

b   About _____ known animal and plant species in New Zealand are on the danger list.

c   Foot-and-mouth disease is about the most _____ disease known because it can be so easily carried.

d   Specially trained _____ dogs work at airports to stop unwanted organisms getting in.

Minerals

As well as coal, oil and gas, New Zealand has a lot of minerals.

A mineral is a substance with a chemical make-up, found in the Earth's surface.

Many New Zealand minerals are mined to be used in all sorts of things such as paints, plastics, paper, cloth, rubber, medicine, concrete, tiles, pottery, bricks, glass, fertiliser, roads, electronics, glues. Dolomite, for example, is used in harbour protection blocks, zeolite in animal litter.

New Zealand soils do not have enough of some necessary minerals. Lack of cobalt causes bush sickness in animals. Lack of selenium is thought to lower good health in humans. Farmers add minerals to the soil.

Examples of New Zealand's metallic minerals

gold (a famous gold mine is Martha Mine at Waihi in the Coromandel)

ilmenite (West Coast of South Island)

iron (from black sands of west coast beaches between Greymouth and Westport in South Island and from Wanganui to Muriwai in North Island)

silver (mostly from Coromandel with gold)

platinum (in Southland)

others manganese, base metals (copper, lead, zinc), iron ore, stibnite (antimony), orpiment (arsenic), chromite, monazite (rare earths), nickel, rutile, tin, bauxite, cinnabar (of mercury)

Examples of New Zealand's non-metallic minerals

aggregates (throughout NZ)

clays (throughout NZ; include bentomite, halloysite, kaolinite)

limestone (throughout NZ)

silica sand (Northland, North Auckland)

zeolite (Ngakuru in central North Island)

serpentine (Wairere in Northland and Greenhills in Southland)

dolomite (near Collingwood)

greenstone/nephrite/pounamu (in north Westland and northern Fiordland)

salt (Lake Grassmere in Marlborough)

sulphur (Rotokawa near Taupo)

others diatomite, barite, feldspar, magnesite, mica, phosphate, wollastonite

1   Write the missing mineral into the spaces in the following sentences.

a   The two main minerals mined in the Coromandel are _____ and _____.

b   Bush sickness is caused by lack of _____ in the soil.

c   The colour of ironsands is _____.

d   The mineral on this page with the most letters in its name is _____.

e   The mineral mined at Lake Grassmere is _____.

f   The mineral used in animal litter is _____.

g   A mineral used to make harbour protection blocks is _____.

h   The Māori word for greenstone is _____.

i   Three non-metallic minerals found throughout New Zealand are _____, _____, and _____.

j   Orpiment is also known as _____.

k   Antimony is also known as _____.

Exports

export – to earn money by sending goods to other countries

In recent years the most valuable exports have been (in order of most valuable first):
* dairy produce, eggs and honey
* meat and edible offal (products like the heart and kidneys of an animal)
* logs, wood and wood articles.

Other main exports are:
* fish, crustaceans (have two pairs of feelers e.g. shrimp) and molluscs (have a shell e.g. oyster)
* mechanical machinery
* aluminium and articles
* fruit and nuts
* wool
* electrical machinery
* raw hides, skins, leather
* paper and paperboard
* iron and steel and articles
* mineral fuels
* textiles (woven fabrics) and articles

New Zealand's export trade is set to do well because of the growing world demand for our organic produce.

In recent years these have been the top 20 countries for New Zealand's exports.

1 Australia		11 Singapore	
2 China		12 Malaysia	
3 USA		13 Philippines	
4 Japan		14 Thailand	
5 United Kingdom		15 Germany	
6 South Korea		16 Saudi Arabia	
7 Indonesia		17 Canada	
8 India		18 Netherlands	
9 Hong Kong		19 Venezuela	
10 Taiwan		20 France	

1 Colour the countries' boxes – red = American; blue = Asian; yellow = NZ's closest neighbour; green = European; orange = Middle East.

2 After the following exports write the official term each export would be named under.

a sheep hair _____   **b** mussels _____

c crabs _____   **d** woven scarves _____

e butter _____   **f** yoghurt _____

3 Write in the 'boxes' the names of the three most valuable exports for a recent year.

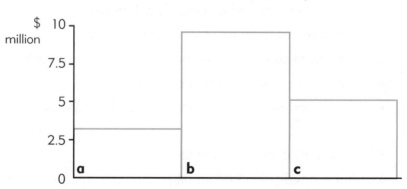

New Zealand's most valuable exports

$ million (y-axis: 0, 2.5, 5, 7.5, 10) — bars labelled a, b, c

Imports

import – to bring goods in from another country

In recent years these have been the top 20 countries for New Zealand's imports:

1 Australia
2 China
3 USA
4 Japan
5 Germany
6 Singapore
7 Malaysia
8 South Korea
9 Thailand
10 United Kingdom

11 United Arab Emirates
12 Qatar
13 Taiwan
14 Italy
15 Indonesia
16 Brunei
17 France
18 Canada
19 Russia
20 India

Some of New Zealand's main imports:

1 mechanical machinery ☐
2 vehicles, parts and accessories ☐
3 electrical machinery ☐
4 textiles and articles ☐
5 mineral fuels ☐
6 plastic and articles ☐
7 aircraft and parts ☐
8 optical, medical equipment ☐
9 paper and paperboard ☐
10 iron and steel and articles ☐
11 pharmaceutical products ☐
12 inorganic chemicals ☐
13 books, newspapers, magazines ☐
14 chemical products ☐
15 rubber and articles ☐

 1 Write down the names of countries that appear on the import list but not on the export list.

 2 Write down the names of countries that appear on the export list but not on the import list.

 3 Tick the boxes that are beside the name of an import which also appears on the list of exports.

Resource Management Act

Resources are the things that make New Zealand wealthy or help it make money. Rivers, lakes, land, fish, oil, coal, coasts, geothermal areas, soils, forests, farmland and air are examples of resources.

To make sure such resources don't run out or get damaged while people are using them, Parliament makes laws to help people use the resources sensibly. This is resource management.

The most important law is the Resource Management Act (RMA). It is all about looking after and managing New Zealand's land, air and water resources. These are natural resources, put here by nature for everyone to enjoy. It lets local places have a big say in what goes on there, rather than making one law for all places.

The RMA wants people, as far as possible, to make their own choices about how they use and protect resources.

It wants to get people to think of possible results of their plan of action. For example, if you wanted to build a golf-course beside an estuary full of mangroves and native birds, you need to think about what could happen to the mangroves and birds. If you wanted to build a tourist lodge in a wilderness area, you need to think about what could happen to the trees, the river and the animals there.

 1 Put a green circle around the names of natural resources in the box and a red circle around threats to those resources.

pollution	wetland	air	mountain	new wharf	soil	unfenced stock
river	new subdivision	factory discharge	kiwi	area of native bush		
coast	coal	forestry	mining	harbour dredging	farm runoff	
underground water	lake	sewage	depot of now outlawed farm chemicals			
geyser	landfill	island	permits to use river for irrigation	hot spring		

2 Write down which word in 'Resource Management Act' best fits the following descriptions.

a A law passed by Parliament _____

b Controlling the use of something properly _____

c Gifts of nature that can be used by people _____

9780170217798

UNIT
43

The heartland

The heartland of a country is its centre. Many people think of it as being smaller and rural, away from major airports and motorways, where life is perhaps not as rushed as in cities. Heartland carries the idea that these places have been important in the development of the country.

Taihape is on the southern edge of the volcanic plateau. Close to Rangitikei River and Ruahine Ranges, it is popular with hunters and trampers. It services high country sheep and deer farms, and is known as the Gumboot Capital of the World. It used to be a main railway marshalling yard with many railway houses.

The small service town of Omarama is near the southern end of the Mackenzie Basin near many rivers and lakes. It attracts gliders, anglers, skiers, trampers and artists. When wool and sheep meat prices dropped many farms changed to dairying. Tussock became pasture with large irrigation systems. Some farmers now plant oilseed rape for biofuel.

Tokoroa is in Waikato, near the Mamaku Ranges and many lakes. It serviced farmers who struggled as soil lacked cobalt which caused animals to waste away with bush sickness. Forestry pines were planted and when Kinleith Mill opened, workers settled in Tokoroa through which the railway passed. Recently much forest has changed into dairy farms.

Examples of New Zealand's heartland

Reefton is a small town on the West Coast in a valley of the Inangahua River. It was the first in NZ and the Southern Hemisphere to get electricity. Its name came from gold found in a quartz reef and the town serviced goldmining. There is still gold-mining there, along with coalmining, forestry, tourism and angling. Most traffic on its railway today is coal.

Te Kuiti is a small service town in the King Country, in south Waikato. It is on the North Island Main Trunk Railway in a valley of limestone deposits. The Mangaokewa stream runs through it. Known as the Sheep-shearing Capital of the world, it hosts the National Shearing Championships. The steep hilly area has mainly farms and limestone quarries.

Gore is in Southland on the banks of Mataura River. A service town for farms, its population dropped when farming declined. Businesses such as its 100-year-old cereal mill closed. Recently many farms have changed to dairying which has helped revive the town. The railway still runs through town although passenger services have stopped.

1 ▶ Draw arrows from the boxes to the map to show where the towns are located.

2 ▶ Give features that most or all the named towns have in common.

a location _____

b size _____

c waterways _____

d reason for township _____

e early transport system _____

Underwater New Zealand

When you look at New Zealand on a map it is just a group of islands in the South Pacific. You can't see much of New Zealand because a lot of it is under the water.

New Zealand is surrounded by a **continental shelf**. This is gently-sloping seabed that gets to about 100 – 160 metres deep. It varies in width. For example, it is only a few hundred metres in Fiordland but in the western Cook Strait it is over 100 km.

In the last ice-age of 20,000 years ago, much of the world's water was frozen in polar ice-caps so the sea was much lower. What is now New Zealand's continental shelf was then a plain. New Zealand's three main islands were joined together. Waikato River flowed north and entered the sea at the eastern side of the North Island.

New Zealand is part of **Zealandia**, the New Zealand continent, which was part of the former supercontinent **Gondwana**. Most of Zealandia is under the water. New Zealand is the largest part of it above water. The next largest part is New Caledonia.

Zealandia is almost half the size of Australia. It stretches from New Caledonia in the north to past New Zealand's **subantarctic** islands (Antipides Islands, Auckland Islands, Bounty Islands, Campbell Islands, the Snares) in the south.

Scientists say most of the world's **volcanism** is in the ocean. For example, the **Kermadec Arc**, stretching north-east of New Zealand, has about 90 volcanoes. Most are underwater with only Kermadec Island above sea level.

Scientists use mini-submarines to explore New Zealand's underwater area. The subs can go down 1,900 m and stay for up to 10 hours. They have **robotic arms** to take samples. Who knows exactly what resources they might find? Maybe natural gas, gold, ironsand, ferromanganese and volcanic sulphides. For example, New Zealand's large gasfield, at Taranaki, is in Zealandia.

1 ▷ Put the orange bold words beside their meanings.

a the New Zealand continent _____

b about volcanoes and their actions _____

c non-human limbs _____

d the submerged crust of a land mass _____

e a region immediately north of Antarctica _____

f former supercontinent _____

g a Pacific region containing a volcanic system _____

2 ▷ Name five resources that scientists may discover in New Zealand's underwater area.

_____ _____

_____ _____

_____

Gateway to Antarctica

The city has a statue of Robert Falcon Scott who sailed from Lyttelton to the ice and never came back.

The university has the Gateway Antarctica Centre for Antarctic Studies and researches climate change and engineering in extreme environments.

Overseas passengers disembark through air-bridge that has large images of Antarctica and emperor penguins with sound effects.

Christchurch is the official gateway to Antarctica, 4,000kms away.

Over 75 percent of world scientists flying to Antarctica leave from here.

Lyttelton continues to be a refuelling station for Antarctic supply vessels.

During Antarctic flying season (usually August to February) military aircraft make about 100 flights to Antarctica from here with passengers and cargo. Trip takes about 5 hours in US Air Force C-17 Globe-master or 7 hours in RNZAF C-130 Hercules.

Home to Antarctic research offices of NZ, US, Italy.

Museums, libraries and the university have Antarctic-related items such as aircraft used in early missions.

US donated Indian totem pole of friendship to airport as thanks for hospitality given to people of Operation Deep Freeze.

Botanic Gardens' Magnetic Observatory helped early explorers locate South Magnetic Pole.

Airport's International Antarctic Centre is major tourist attraction.

Royal NZ Air Force, Air National Guard & US Air Force stationed here as part of Operation Deep Freeze.

Antarctic festivals held there focus on international cooperation, research, technology, climate change, environment, future.

Art Gallery Te Puna O Waiwhetu shows works from the Artists in Antarctica programme which involves artists spending up to 3 weeks at Scott Base.

1 Name eight physical signs of the link between Christchurch and Antarctica.

_____   _____
_____   _____
_____   _____
_____   _____

2 Name the following.

a A famous Antarctic explorer _____

b A famous Antarctic resident _____

c A famous Antarctic research facility _____

d A famous codename for US Antarctic missions _____

e A famous port for Antarctic-bound vessels _____

Northern tourist hotspots

Tongaririo Crossing: In Tongariro National Park volcanic plateau. Near active Mt Ruapehu, periodically steaming Mt Ngauruhoe, dormant Mt Tongariro. Lava sculptures, cliffs, geothermal areas, lakes, crater floor, hot springs, native bush.

Mt Tarawera: 1886 eruption killed over 150, destroyed world-famous Pink and White Terraces, buried villages under volcanic mud, created or changed many Rotorua lakes that surround it.

Cape Reinga: At tip of Aupouri Peninsula. Regarded as place where Tasman Sea to west meets Pacific Ocean to east. North Cape's Surville Cliffs to east are slightly further north.

Coromandel Peninsula: Widest point is 40 kms. Hilly, steep, much subtropical rainforest. Coromandel Range rises to nearly 900 m. Offshore islands e.g. Slipper, Aldermans, Mercury Islands.

Waipoua Kauri Forest: Northland. Kauri remains of ancient subtropical rainforest. Some named e.g. Tane Mahuta (Lord of the Forest), over 51 m high, estimated to be 1,250 – 2,500 years old.

White Island/ Whakaari: Off coast of Bay of Plenty. Active volcano considered to be most accessible on planet. Part of Taupo Volcanic Zone. Roughly circular. Much of it underwater. Peak is 321 m above sea level.

Waitomo Caves: In Waikato. Story began over 30 million years ago when limestone was created at bottom of ocean. Today limestone formations and cave systems lit by thousands of a type of glow worm unique to NZ.

Lake Taupo: Deep point 186 m. Perimeter about 193 km. Drained by Waikato River. Trout fishery. Lies in caldera (like a crater) created by supervolcanic eruption about 26,500 years ago, one of largest in recorded history.

Rotorua: On volcanic plateau. Sulfur City (hydrogen sulfide emissions), Rotovegas (many motels and neon signs like US Las Vegas). Geothermal activity such as Pohutu Geyser at Whakarewarewa and hot mud pools.

Mt Taranaki: One of most evenly-shaped volcanic cones in world. Young, started activity about 135,000 years ago. Minor eruptions about every 90 years on average and major eruptions every 500 years.

1 ▸ Draw arrows from the box to its location on the map.

2 ▸ Name the different types of natural features mentioned on this page.

_____

_____

_____

_____

9780170217798

Southern tourist hotspots

Lake Wanaka: In Otago, just north of Queenstown. Town in glacier carved basin on lake shores, gateway to Mt Aspiring National Park. Tourism is new gold for old goldmining area.

Franz Josef and Fox Glaciers: In Westland Tai Poutini National Park. Unique as descend from Southern Alps to less than 300 m above sea level in middle of rainforest and temperate (mild rather than extreme climate) environment.

Fiordland: In south-western corner. Steep sides of Southern Alps, ocean-flooded valleys. Has Milford Sound, NZ's deepest lakes (Te Anau, Hauroko, Manapouri), 2 of world's tallest waterfalls (Browne, Sutherland).

Moeraki Boulders (Kaihinaki): Just south of Oamaru on east coast. Maybe about 60 million years old. Round stones on beach. Some up to 4 m in circumference. Created by process similar to formation of oyster pearls.

Queenstown: In Otago at inlet of long, thin Lake Wakatipu, by Remarkables. Centre for adventure tourism e.g. skiing, heli skiing, boating, bungy, fly fishing, mountain biking, white water rafting.

Aoraki/Mt Cook: In Aoraki/ Mt Cook National Park in Mackenzie area of Southern Alps. 3 summits: Low Peak, Middle Peak, High Peak. Tasman Glacier to east, Hooker Glacier to west.

Kaikoura: Seaward Kaikoura mountains, branch of Southern Alps at northern end almost meeting the sea. Whale watching, swimming with or near dolphins. Colony of southern fur seals. Seabirds e.g. albatross, petrel.

Milford Sound (Piopiotahi): Within Fiordland National Park. Has won world's top travel destination in survey. Runs 15 km inland from Tasman Sea at Dale Point. Has Mitre Peak.

Punakaiki Pancake Rocks: At Dolomite Point on West Coast. Eroded limestone; sea bursts through blowholes. Pancake layering created by great pressure on alternating hard and soft layers of animal and plant remains.

Ulva Island: In Paterson Inlet, part of Stewart Island/Rakirua. About 3.5 km long area of about 270 hectares. Sanctuary for endangered plants and birds e.g. kaka, yellow-eyed penguin, rifleman, brown kiwi.

1 Name the places shown in the photos.

_____

_____

2 Name two features the hotspots have in common. _____

_____

Examples of New Zealand's world-famous ski areas and beaches	
Anaura Bay near Gisborne	Awana Bay on Great Barrier Island
Broken River in Craigieburn Forest Park	Cardrona near Wanaka
Cathedral Cove in Coromandel	Coopers in Coromandel
Coronet Peak by Queenstown	Craigieburn in Craigieburn Forest Park
Hanmer Springs on Mt St Patrick	Hot Water in Coromandel
Kaiteriteri in Nelson Bays in Canterbury	Karekare west of Auckland
Makoriri at Gisborne	Manganui at Mt Taranaki
Manu Bay at Raglan	Mission Bay in Auckland
Mt Cheeseman near Christchurch	Mt Dobson near Queenstown
Mt Lyford in Canterbury	Mt Hutt near Christchurch
Mt Maunganui in Bay of Plenty	Mt Olympus in Craigieburn Range
Mt Potts in Two Thumb and Cloudy Peak	90 Mile in Northland
Ohau in Mackenzie country south of Twizel	Onetangi Bay on Waikehe Island
Opunake on Surf Highway Taranaki-Whanganui	Piha west of Auckland
Porter Heights near Porters Pass	Rainbow near St Arnaud
Roundhill near Lake Tekapo	St Clair in Dunedin
Sumner at Christchurch	Takapuna in Auckland
Taylors Mistake on Banks Peninsula	Temple Basin in Arthur's Pass National Park
The Remarkables across from Coronet Peak	Treble Cone by Wanaka
Waiorau in Cardrona Valley	Wenderholm north of Waiwera
Whakapapa and Turoa at Ruapehu	Wharariki by Farewell Spit

1 Use the location of each ski area or beach to help you do the following.

a Highlight the ski areas in yellow. (21) **b** Highlight the beaches in blue. (21)

2 Use the photos to help you name the following.

a A 'must visit' gigantic arched cavern _____

b The alpine resort often called Adventure Capital of the World _____

c West of Auckland and popular with experienced surfers _____

National cycle trail

The idea for New Zealand's National Cycle Trail (Nga Haerenga) came out of a 2009 job summit. Government later approved millions of dollars for a series of 'Great Rides'.

Some aims were to
- provide world-class cycle trails
- showcase New Zealand's spectacular scenery
- promote the '100% Pure New Zealand' tourist brand
- attract more international tourists
- provide cycle experiences for Kiwis
- encourage a healthy activity
- help struggling small towns by bringing tourists to them
- provide jobs for people building the trails
- provide business opportunities for locals such as bed and breakfast
- provide tracks that children and locals could also use to and from school and work.

Example: Kumara on the West Coast used to be a goldmining centre but now has only a few hundred people left. The Westland Wilderness Cycle Trail could bring tourists to the area.

The first to be officially opened, in 2010, was the St James Cycle Trail near Hanmer Springs and surrounded by Molesworth Station. It was different to other national trails because it was designed to suit advanced bikers only. The 64–87 km (depending on the circuit you choose) trail takes one to three days and includes steep slopes, river crossings, native beech, scrub, matagouri, tussock, bone-crunching riverbed, swing bridges, switchbacks and climbs and descents of spurs and saddles.

1 Use the photo to give reasons why New Zealand attracts biking tourists.

a _____

_____

b _____

_____

c _____

_____

2 Give benefits to New Zealand of the national cycling trails.

a _____

b _____

c _____

The value of the environment

Nobody can put an exact price on what the environment is worth to New Zealand, but surveys have looked at three export sectors — dairy, tourism, organic food – to try to get a good idea.

Agriculture has always been a large earner of export dollars. Surveys show that New Zealand's customers take notice of the clean, green image. They like to see food being produced in a natural environment.

Organic food is becoming a big market in areas like the UK and Europe, where food scares such as an *E-coli* poisoning in 2011 in Germany make consumers think more about what they eat and how it has been produced.

Tourism is another large earner. New Zealand advertises itself to overseas tourists as clean and green which suggests its food is safe to eat, its water is safe to drink, its ocean is safe to swim in, its air is safe to breathe, and that it's a place where you can see native animals and plants in their native habitats and people happily make a living while looking after the environment. Overseas tourists are attracted to this idea of an unspoiled paradise.

The surveys show that if the environment was seen to be damaged, it would have a huge effect on the New Zealand economy. Exporters would be more cautious of buying New Zealand products, and tourists would be more cautious about visiting. Once this had happened it would be hard to regain the clean, green image – probably harder than fixing the environment.

By world standards New Zealand is fairly clean and green although it has environmental problems it needs to fix before the image gets badly dented. Examples are air quality in Christchurch and Auckland, and pollution of rivers and the ocean.

New Zealand has the means, such as the Resource Management Act and the Hazardous Substances and New Organisms Act, to keep the environment clean. Positive action has already happened such as developing food safety systems. These actions have dollar value for export markets.

> **1** Use the photo to help name the following.

a The mountain. _____

b The type of agriculture. _____

c Three export sectors interested in this type of scene. _____

_____ _____

d The result on the economy if this location was found to be polluted.

_____

e The image New Zealand wants to sell to export markets.

_____

f Two Acts of Parliament aimed to protect the environment.

_____ _____

Why New Zealand is special

New Zealand's spectacular scenery is becoming popular with movie makers. They know that in a country like USA they can travel for days or weeks and see nothing but the same sort of scenery all the time. In New Zealand they can see different types in the space of a few hours.

Westland's Lake Matheson has picture perfect reflections making it one of the most photographed lakes anywhere.

It is not over-populated.

While many other countries are chopping down their rainforest, NZ sets much of its forest aside as parks. Milford Track (54 km) is said to be the finest walk in the world.

Waitomo Caves is one of the great underground wonders of the world.

New Zealand is often called God's Own Country and the Paradise of the Pacific. It wins awards for being the best country in the world to visit.

A hill near Porangahau in Hawke's Bay is said to be the world's longest real name. Taumatawhakatangiha ngakoauauatamateapokai whenuakitangatahu means 'the summit of the hill where Tamatea the traveller played the flute to his beloved.'

NZ has some amazing wildlife that often makes international news. Its black robin was once the rarest bird in the world but has been snatched from extinction. The Kiwi occurs only in New Zealand. A small colony of takahe was found in Fiordland 50 years after the bird was thought to be extinct.

Stewart Island's Māori name is Rakiura, which means 'island of glowing skies'. Rangitoto Island, NZ's newest volcano, is a symbol of Auckland's wonderful harbour. World-famous environmentalist Jacques Cousteau described the Poor Knights Islands, off Northland's coast, as one of the world's top ten dives.

wide open spaces
clean and green
islands
golden beaches
luxuriant forests
petrified (turned to stone) forest
snow-capped mountains
waterfalls
lava flows
hot springs
desert road through a volcanic plateau
geysers and mudpools
whales, dolphins, seals, sea lions
wild horses
strange rock shapes
drowned river valleys
alpine herbfields
snowfields
glaciers, glacier lakes
limestone canyons
underwater streams
blowholes
wild coasts
woolly sheep

1 Give the terms for each of the following that a movie maker could find in New Zealand.

a   a sea version of a volcano _____

b   a forest that has turned to stone _____

c   three birds _____, _____, and

_____

d   the 'finest walking track in the world' _____

e   one of the world's top 10 dives _____

f   the English name for Rakiura _____

g   the meaning of Rakiura _____

h   Westland's photographed lake _____

i   one of the underground wonders in the world _____

2 Write down a number for the following.

Taumatawhakatangihangakoauauotamateaturipukakapikimaungahoronukupokaiwhenuakitanatahu

a   letters in New Zealand's longest place name _____

b   places in New Zealand named on this page _____

Final challenge

1   A large unbroken land mass is called a _____.

2   New Zealand lies in the _____ Ocean.

3   The nickname for the Tasman Sea between New Zealand and Australia is

_____.

4   New Zealand is in the _____ Hemisphere.

5   Bluff is at the bottom of the _____ Island.

6   The cape with the lighthouse at the top of the North Island is Cape _____.

7   The strait between the North and the South Island is called _____ Strait.

8   The strait between the South Island and Stewart Island is called _____

Strait.

9   The islands belonging to New Zealand east of Christchurch are called the

_____ Islands.

10 Of New Zealand's three main islands, the largest is called the _____

Island.

11 Of New Zealand's three main islands, the smallest is called _____

Island.

12 The highest mountain is Aoraki/Mount _____.

13 The Tokelau Islands are looked after by the country of _____.

14 90 Mile Beach is in the north of the _____ Island.

15 The gulf around Auckland is called the _____ Gulf.

16 Most of New Zealand's kiwifruit comes from the Bay of _____.

17 The main gas and oil fields are in the _____ region.

18 Hamilton is in the _____ Island.

19 Timaru is in the _____ Island.

20 Nelson is in the _____ Island.

21 Christchurch is in the _____ Island.

22 Wellington is in the _____ Island.

23 New Zealand's population is about 4.4 _____.

24 The average number of people living in a square kilometre is known as _____.

25 The coldest month is normally the month of _____.

26 Another term for the greenhouse effect or climate change is _____

warming.

27 There is an _____ smelter at Tiwai Point.

28 Nga Haerenga is the name of New Zealand's national _____.

29 The famous tunnel near Milford Sound is called the _____ Tunnel.

9780170217798

30 A piece of land like Coromandel which is almost surrounded by water is called a
_____.

31 A lake in a valley is called a _____ lake.

32 A narrow way through a mountain range is called a _____.

33 Ka Tiritiri o te Moana is Māori for the _____.

34 The longest glacier is called _____.

35 The Catlins mountain range is in the _____ Island.

36 The Canterbury _____, a large flat land area, is the largest in New Zealand.

37 The largest lake is called Lake _____.

38 The Rangitaiki River is in the _____ Island.

39 The Clutha River is in the _____ Island.

40 The famous tourist town on Lake Wakatipu is called _____.

41 Fauna means all the _____ of a country.

42 Flora means all the _____ of a country.

43 Stoats were introduced to control _____.

44 The biggest insect in the world is New Zealand's _____.

45 _____ dolphin is the smallest and rarest marine dolphin in the world.

46 The tree known as the King of the Forest is the _____.

47 The tree that Project Crimson is trying to save is the _____.

48 Bio_____ means keeping living things safe from unwanted organisms entering New Zealand.

49 The disease which Britain had in 2001 and which caused a scare in New Zealand was
_____.

50 Sedimentary, igneous and metamorphic are types of _____.

51 Land suitable for cultivation is known as a_____ land.

52 The tree most planted for forestry is called _____.

53 Exotic forest means forest that was put there by _____.

54 Indigenous forest means forest that has been put there by _____.

55 New Zealand has _____ World Heritage areas, a big number for a small country.

56 The measurement used for land is _____.

57 Queen _____ Sound is in Marlborough.

58 Aoraki is the Māori name for _____.

59 Planting trees is good for the environment because they _____.

60 New Zealand's Exclusive Economic Zone extends for _____ miles.

61 Large prawns and shrimps are known as _____.

62 In extensive pastoralism the farms and stations are _____ in size.

63 The measurement used to describe farm size is _____.

64 Cropping and horticulture are found on _____ land rather than hilly land or highland.

65 The cultivation of fruit, vegetables and flowers is known as _____.

66 Industry which gathers raw materials, such as mining, is known as _____ industry.

67 A person who travels for pleasure is known as a _____.

68 Energy that renews itself such as hydro, is known as _____ energy.

69 Viticulture means the _____ industry.

70 The fruit that ZESPRI markets is called _____.

71 New Zealand's oil refinery is at _____ Point.

72 Solar energy comes from the _____.

73 The type of energy produced at Wairakei is called _____.

74 The main mineral mined at Martha Mine in Waihi is _____.

75 _____ is produced at Lake Grassmere.

76 Goods sent overseas from New Zealand to earn money are called _____.

77 Goods bought by New Zealand from other countries are called _____.

78 A crab, but not a snapper, is called a mollusc because it has a _____.

79 The 'Ring of fire' means that area is likely to have volcanic eruptions and _____.

80 A natural hazard is a danger made by _____.

81 _____ Island is a volcanic island off the coast of the Bay of Plenty.

82 Too much uncontrolled fast-moving water is called a _____.

83 Tephra is material produced by a _____.

84 The inter-island ferry *Wahine* sank in _____ Harbour.

85 The largest volcanic eruption anywhere in the world was from _____.

86 Earthquakes are measured on the R_____ Scale.

87 The mountain that exploded in 1886 was Mount _____.

88 In 1931 Napier suffered a big _____.

89 Not enough water for the land is known as a _____.

90 The most common natural hazard is _____.

91 A _____ is strong winds with rain, hail, or snow.

92 A narrow funnel of violently spinning air is called a _____.

93 Typhoon and hurricane are other terms for a _____.

94 Tsunami is the Japanese word for a _____.

95 Abbotsford is a suburb of the city of _____.

96 Things such as water and coal which help make New Zealand wealthy, are called r_____.

97 Rangitoto Island is in _____ Harbour.

98 Matheson is the name of a much-photographed _____.

99 One of the great dives in the world is at the _____ Knights Islands.

100 _____ Caves is one of the great underground wonders of the world.

9780170217798